Dr. Patricia J. Vanderpool is a bright newcomer to the writing world. She possesses the ability to maintain the attention and interest of both seasoned and new readers alike. She genuinely cares about her writing and the readers who enjoy her work. She is passionate, witty, articulate and insightful. The author writes as though she will be reading and enjoying the book herself. She tries to maintain a standard of excitement and intelligence in her writing. Patricia writes to and for both male and female readers alike, piquing interest with an intense and dynamic nature to her writing.

I had thought nothing about dedicating this book to anyone before being asked. After much thought, I believe I will in fact dedicate it to my parents: William (Bill) and Elizabeth Vanderpool for being normal, hardworking folks.

Dr. Patricia J. Vanderpool

ABSOLUTELY DESPICABLE!

AUSTIN MACAULEY PUBLISHERS™

LONDON • CAMBRIDGE • NEW YORK • SHARJAH

A CIP catalogue record for this title is available from the British Library.

ISBN 9781528994248 (Paperback)
ISBN 9781528994255 (Hardback)
ISBN 9781528994262 (ePub e-book)
ISBN 9781398437678 (Audiobook)

www.austinmacauley.com

First Published 2022
Austin Macauley Publishers Ltd®
1 Canada Square
Canary Wharf
London
E14 5AA

I would like to acknowledge each person who shared their story with me.

Table of Contents

Real stories and life-altering events expose the corrupt
nature of a small town.

It's not just someone else's problem!

Culture and experience shape each of us. Each of us then cause change, practice influence, and promote thought and action among those we are in contact with daily. Even a targeted self-indulgent action will produce a ripple effect that has the potential to last a lifetime. The people who are sharing their stories in this book are doing so to bring light to the brazen actions that get swept under the rug all too often. It might not be you today, but it very well could be you or your loved ones on the receiving end of injustice tomorrow.

Introduction

As Doctor of Nursing Practice (DNP) with an elite and dynamic education from some of the best institutions across the United States, I am fortunate enough to be able to help open the eyes of injustice for regular folks. I am certified by the American Nurses Credentialing Centre (ANCC) in both family and adult (internal) practice. In my daily practice as primary care provider, part of my job is to listen, support and advocate for my patients. I not only treat their physical ailments, but also practice in a holistic manner to treat the entire being. I continuously practice the art of listening with my patients; sometimes to be heard is all they need. Often times, just listening to the frustration patients are burdened with allows me to really get to the root of a problem. I not only help with illness, I am also fortunate enough to help with life.

Prologue

This Book Is Based on True Events

The names in the stories that will follow have been changed to protect both the innocent and the guilty.

Enclosed are real stories of people who have been victim of and affected by abuse, neglect and corruption including death and probable cover-up of murder.

Imagine if you will, an uneducated small-town sheriff who is presumed to be homosexual, deciding your life is worth nothing! You are less than he believes himself to be because you are a young gay man of only 19, who spent ten or so years in foster care programs in Indiana. You, with a tragic upbringing that includes being beaten by a drunken father on a routine basis. Provided very little to eat by the same man who consequently marks the milk jug every night with a sharpie and counts each slice of bologna and bread as he designates one slice a day to each of his six children; the remaining meals you get are served at school as free breakfast and lunch. You have very little support, either family or social. Your siblings are also beaten and starved on a regular basis, each with no one to turn to when in need emotionally, mentally, or physically. Your predator knows your situation.

He feels he is safe in his position as sheriff deputy and pounces on you, blood-thirsty.

Unlawful fraternisation with inmates of the Henry County Jail, resulting in the birth of a child. This person went on to become sheriff of Henry County Indiana with as little as 2400 or so votes. The past behaviour of these individuals is more than likely why there have been multiple deaths, drugs, drug overdose, and corruption in the Henry County Jail for years.

A past chief of police leaving town without packing and never coming back! Why leave your home and all your personal belongings to only tell people later how corrupt the town is? Why would you not do anything about it except go along with it when you had the chance, unless you had something to gain by the corruption. This is an example of the small-mindedness that plagues the city of New Castle, Indiana, and has for years.

Stupidity amplified in the powers that be; deception and schemes related to federal grant money. All this taking place in small-town USA where they think they can get away with it because it has been going on for so long. Suddenly, grant signs everywhere, supposed grant money poured into a dead downtown. Despite all this supposed upgrade and spent money, nothing has changed. Empty store fronts line run-down streets, rundown buildings, and vacant property. Did this grant money line the pockets of local officials as suspected by many residents. It's obvious it did not promote a major upgrade in downtown New Castle, Indiana, as it was designated to do.

A place where the mentality is so warped, they are amused by a wild turkey on the main highway that seems to wander in and out of traffic. Instead of the local wild-life or humane society protecting and trying to remove this animal from harm, they make a wild turkey a celebrity. This animal was killed in traffic; negligence and ignorance again prevailed. A makeshift memorial with stove-top stuffing placed as a marker is a cruel injustice to wild animals and speaks to the unkind nature and obliviousness that abounds in New Castle, Indiana. This is not entertainment, this is inhumane and idiocy!

You will be privy to the local good old boy network to get what you want and avoid punishment for crimes that include attempted stabbing as well as police harassment, targeting and property destruction. The misuse of power within this small town is discussed including avoidance of punishment because you are related to or friends of the local sheriff or judge and presume yourself to be above the law. A judge who, for a tryst, will dismiss a woman's child support, drunk driving offenses, and drug mishaps!

Multiple types of abuse are exposed in this book. Stories and encounters of elderly abuse, battered women, and alcoholic fits of rage from the folks that endured or witnessed this horrific behaviour. People who want and need to be heard to begin the healing process and possibly prevent further devastating events from taking place. Folks just wanting someone or everyone to know how they were treated, mistreated, abused, and the injustice of it all.

You will be entertained and amused by witticisms and anecdotes, tragedy, and amazing stories of the will to survive. It is hard to believe these types of things are going on right under our noses. Nonetheless, in the societal rush to get things done as quickly as possible, we pay no attention to our surroundings, our neighbours, our friends, or those that are supposed to be practicing maleficence in our communities. The attitude of let someone else deal with it too often prevails in the world today.

We no longer vote thinking it makes no difference, but the power you possess to educate and influence others could make all the difference. If you're tired of the status quo, then step up! Use the stories and events of this book as enlightenment to make changes when they are needed.

I hope you enjoy reading this book as much as I have enjoyed writing it. I was the victim of police targeting and harassment. I spent 7 days in the local jail for driving my car! I was exposed to more drugs and perversion in the Henry County Indiana Jail than on the street. I was also accosted by a man in a manic type rage. This man yielded a knife, lunging at me and my 10-pound rescued puppy who were out for a walk. The local sheriff's department did nothing because this criminal assailant was friends with Deputy Moore of the Henry County Sheriff's Department. These people did not and do not care. It's easy for them to lie and cover up because it has happened so often in Henry County Indiana. It's personal for me and it better be personal for you too; whose friend will accost you and get away with it?

Chapter 1

The Possible Murder Cover-Up of Curtis Wagner

Did a Henry County Indiana Sheriff get away with murder? Curtis Wagner's brother, Ronnie Wagner, gives total written permission to include him and his story in this project and brings additional information to the project regarding suspected foul play in his brother Curtis' demise. These names are also real as Ronnie Wagner wants to spread awareness of how bad the brutality and cover-up really is. The nature of Curtis' death has had a profound effect on Ronnie's life; mentally, he lost part of his own life and future because of this horrific incident. Ronnie approached telling me of Curtis' death as the cause for his mental breakdown and the reason he is on disability today for mental illness and post-traumatic stress.

He tells me he was imprisoned in 1991 when this incident took place. It depends on your point of view as to how you judge Ronnie and his crime, but again, only you can judge, and this doesn't take away the seriousness of potential murder cover-up. Ronnie's crime was having marijuana in his possession. A crime he was imprisoned for and later we find out a local sheriff's son (Barker) had the same issue and the entire thing was dismissed. This is injustice, prejudice, self-serving, and frankly illegal to all involved in sweeping the young Barker boy's pot bust under the rug in 2017. The only difference in the two is one is a local seemingly crooked sheriff's son and the other is a poor kid with no support from the wrong side of the tracks if you will.

Ronnie says an officer of the local Henry County Sherriff's Department came to the prison where he was being held and gave him a packet of information regarding his brother's death and told him to seek counsel in the form of an attorney. Ronnie's sister now has this packet. This interaction between Ronnie and the deputy can easily be verified by prison records kept of visitors. Ronnie says initially this elicited fear inside because he had only weeks before he was to be released and a visit from a Henry County Sheriff's Deputy was the last thing he expected.

It's apparent by the actions of this deputy that others were aware of the foul play surrounding the death of young Curtis Wagner, and at least had the integrity to step up and make the family aware of this wrongdoing as well as the inappropriate actions taken by the local sheriff department. Ronnie goes on to tell me that a local undertaker, Sham Shall, facilitated the funeral and told him to seek an attorney that his brother was killed by a local sheriff department's employee, Kimberly Clank. Sham told Ronnie that his brother did not get dragged by a train greater than 1000 feet as described by the local sheriff's official Mr Kimberly Clank, but instead was hit in the back of the skull with blunt force causing trauma and death. The trauma to the posterior skull was the only mark on his body. Ronnie says Sham Shall told him there were no other markings on his brother's body, no abrasions, no lacerations, or other wounds of any kind. It would literally be impossible to get dragged more than 1000 feet by a train and not have any outward abrasions, markings or other injuries.

His death certificate from the Henry County, Indiana Health Department dated August 11, 1991 states cause of death: "multiple internal injuries; walking between rails on tracks; struck by train; other conditions". This death certificate was certified by Mark Frame. Documents available in the addendum support foul play and mishandling.

First, it is assumption to say he was "walking between rails on tracks". Let's dissect this for a moment; how do they know he was walking; how do they know it was between the rails; and without autopsy, how do they know internal injuries or the extent thereof of the supposed internal injuries? The only bodily injury visible according to Sham Shall undertaker was a traumatic wound to the back of his head that was not even mentioned on the certificate of death. Next, "other conditions", what does this mean exactly and on a death certificate? This is a generic statement and adds more suspicion to the incident. "Struck by train", OK so how do they know this with a full body intact and no apparent outward injuries or significant markings.

Being hit and dragged more than a thousand feet by a train going normal speed down the tracks, you would expect Curtis' body to be mangled in multiple ways with limbs, hair, skin, blood, and other flesh strewn about up and down the track where this alleged incident occurred. We certainly would not expect to find Curtis' body to be entirely in one neat package with only a posterior head injury. Again, no skid marks, no abrasions, no lacerations, no visible signs of being hit by a train and conflicting stories. When the coroner's report was requested by Ronnie on September 12, 2018, Slacy Gusshy of the local sheriff's department refused to provide one with no explanation why. September 20th, 2018, this was reported to the state coroner's office at the suggestion of the Indiana Attorney General's office; as of today, no reply!

Kimberly Clank is a known homosexual male with some history as an employee of the local sheriff's department, even serving as Sheriff of Henry County Indiana for a while. Guess what, Mr Clank likes to make underground movies for the internet's dark web as it is being told to me by Ronnie Wagner.

Curtis Wagner was a 19-year-old homosexual man/boy who had lived in foster care most of his life after being physically, mentally, and emotionally abused by his father. This abuse included starvation and beatings. It's easy to see psychologically the trust Curtis would have bestowed on Mr Clank, a seemingly trusting authoritative figure. Little did Curtis know Mr Clank's intentions were to sodomise and use him in twisted sexual fantasies. To video tape him dying and cover up his murder for psychotic gratification.

Mr Kimberly Clank did have an accomplice, another gay man who has since died himself. Did Mr Clank's lover get jealous, did he walk in on Mr Clank and young tender Curtis during sodomy and/or oral sex? Did the sight of Curtis' naked body being enjoyed by Mr Clank enrage his lover? Was this enough for the lover Mr Jones to suggest they use Curtis in one of their videos? Curtis could not have known he would be sexually exploited and possibly murdered by the much older and more experienced, supposed to be, but not, benevolent Mr Clank.

This ideology would feed perfectly into the psychotic and hedonistic thoughts of Mr Clank wanting to make an underground movie of murder and death as it unfolds in front of him at his own hand. Subsequently, coincidence or not, another young rumoured gay man, B. Kingsby, was killed the same way on the same train track within a few weeks of Curtis' death. Did Mr Clank think, *Got away with it once, let's do it again*. This would rid him of both young boys he was rumoured to be involved with and allow him to make yet another video of death at his own hands. Was B. Kingsby another victim of Mr Clank?

Neighbours in the Mooreland, Indiana area where Mr Clank resided at the time, are fearful of retaliation and speak of Mr Clank in generalities, with one exception, a female that lived across the street from the house Mr Clank and his male lover occupied. Melba Campus tells another story, the one of Mr Clank and his male accomplice supposedly carrying out the limp and lifeless body of Curtis Wagner, placing it in the trunk of a vehicle parked in the drive at approximately 2am.

After hearing a series of loud noises that had aroused her dog and ultimately awakened Ms Campus, she says she was peering out her front window into the darkness and witnessed Mr Clank place Curtis' lifeless body in the trunk of a car parked in the drive. The same car that Mr Clank drove daily. The street lights of the very small town coupled with the lights of the home Mr Clank occupied, were illumination enough at 2am for Ms Campus to visualise clearly the odd behaviour of the two older men coming and going from the house to the car, seemingly making ready the trunk of Mr Clank's police car. The same police car that would be driven to deposit the lifeless body of Curtis Wagner on the railroad tracks that run along State Road 3 North.

Ms Campus describes her neighbour Mr Clank carrying the limp and lifeless body of polite and timid young Curtis across his arms to the back of the police car. Mr Clank placed Curtis in the trunk and closed the lid. She says Mr Clank did not look back, did not look around, just wiped his hands on his pants as if he was merely playing in dust and ran his hand down his police car as he made his way back up the drive and into the house.

Ms Campus who lived across the street says she often heard the voices of her neighbours yelling and screaming accusations of infidelity, demands to "suck my cock" and threats of death if young Curtis ever gave his love and his body to anyone else. Ms Campus believed Mr Clank was not only taking advantage of young Curtis but exploiting his innocence as well.

Ronnie Wagner's denied pleas to get the police and coroner's reports from the local sheriff department indicate there was something they want to hide and/or someone they want to protect. Is the sheriff's department maintaining a constant state of cover-up, false documentation and lies to allow any behaviour they see fit to take place regardless of the laws everyone else is supposed to abide by? Do they see themselves above the law as they wear a uniform, make judgments of guilt or innocence, and prohibit only what they see as a problem? Not protecting and serving but deceiving, ruining, and taking advantage of a badge and uniform for personal, vindictive, and monetary gain? These people are not qualified to make decisions regarding human life and the will of another; they have very little education and training as evidenced by their actions of disregard, harassment, and favouritism.

This incident was reported to the Indiana State Attorney General and a complaint and request for the coroner report from the state was made. This is obviously foul play, ignorance, cover-up, murder, and not "protect and serve" as you would expect your local sheriff's department to practice. Instead, they practise hedonism at the expense of the public! I was told the last person to pursue this story was threatened, that is why the attorney general was notified of my intent to put the Wagner story in my book.

I have been harassed and jailed by the local sheriff's department for merely driving my car. I was tracked so this made it easy to sneak and ticket me with every opportunity. I received 91 points against my driver's license, lost 2 years of my life that I will never get back, endured the wrongfulness of the local jail for 7 days. Jailed for driving; I repeat, jailed for driving; this only happens when one is harassed. I believe there is a cover-up involving the death of Curtis Wagner and who knows what else for personal gain.

Once again, rumours are flying as now it seems Mr Clank was found dead in his front yard, dying of a self-inflicted gunshot wound. Vindication for Curtis Wagner has finally come, some thirty years later. Mr Clank and another of his lovers, Lagdon Dong, along with another sheriff's deputy and his wife, have been accused and are reportedly being investigated for the videotaping of minors that they have held captive. These young boys have been imprisoned in the Clank home, his own personal jail if you will. Along with Mr Dong, Mr Clank is reported to dress in his old sheriff uniform and beat his young captives, videotaping all the while, exploring and exploiting their young bodies with their tongue, penis, vibrators (typically used by women) and of all things wooden night sticks, all this abuse for personal gratification. Mr Dong with his photographed cigar smoking face, flushed, satisfied and laughing as one of the young boys lay weeping with blood readily flowing from his rectum and another video of a young boy with bruises around his mouth that encompass his nose, chin and cheeks from the oral fuckings he had to repeatedly endure by Mr Dong and Mr Clank. Only to be found out by thinking they could have their computer wiped clean of the videos, pornography and vile actions caught on tape to be re-lived by the two men. Proof when the injuries were too much to simply explain away with a fall or the white lie of a child. Thirty years of these men molesting young boys with troubled pasts who live in poverty in the lower economic areas of the city and surrounding counties where it is rumoured, they would troll for young boys. Sickness hiding behind a so-called boys' camp and taking advantage of the most vulnerable children – absolutely despicable! I was once ticketed by Mr Lagdon, he falsely accused me of doing eighty-two miles an hour around a left-hand turn which is impossible – a liar is a liar, is a liar, and consequently a child molester, pornography master and sodomizer.

Chapter 2

Nadeline, 85 and Abused

Nadeline is a pleasant 85-year-old lady who spent forty years wearing second-hand glasses and living with strangers just to have a roof over her head. She has been influenced and taken advantage of by many of those she came in contact and associated with.

One winter afternoon in January 2017 when there was an abundance of freezing temperatures and snow in central Indiana, Nadeline and the friend she lived with, Vissy, had a fight. This fight ended with Vissy throwing barefooted Nadeline out of the house. Nadeline remembers walking two miles in the freezing snowy weather in only her socks to ask a niece for help. Nadeline had been estranged from her children for almost 40 years. Her children now became her only refuge. She was unsure of their willingness to speak to her, much less help her. With no other choice and no one standing in her way, she reached out to her children and family she had missed and longed for. Until now, she had been under the thumb of Vissy, her supposed caregiver who would take her social security check, spend her money and dictate her actions. She was not free to make her own decisions, speak to her children or handle her own finances.

In Vissy's home, Nadeline was forced to give up her social security check for room and board. Vissy had taken control of Nadeline by becoming her power of attorney via brute force and threats. Vissy opened charge cards in Nadeline's name, had her utilities put in Nadeline's name and spent Nadeline's money as she deemed necessary.

Nadeline was living in a single room in the house that belonged to Vissy and her husband. Vissy was in command of her entire twelve hundred dollar a month social security check. Nadeline was forced to use a bucket as a bathroom for both stool and urine. She was made to keep it in her room, only allowed to come out or empty her refuse bucket once the husband was not at home or in the house. Nadeline was not allowed to shower but had to wash off in a pan of water in her room. She spent twenty years unable to use a proper toilet in a modern home or take a normal bath or shower due to the rules Vissy and her husband had set for her.

Nadeline was forced to sleep in a chair in her bedroom for 20 years, not allowed to have a bed. Vissy refused to give her money that belonged to her to buy herself a proper bed. The utilities and Vissy's credit cards were in Nadeline's name. Nadeline was not allowed to have things of her own. She was allowed two sets of clothes that were worn back and forth from day to day; her clothes had to be hand-washed in the same water she used to bathe and hung in her room to dry. All the while, she was made to do the family laundry with a washer and dryer bought with her money.

She tells me she would wear glasses given to her by Vissy's mother or anyone else who felt pity on her. This is 2017 and these are adults who did not have the compassion, caring or moral institution to help this elderly lady. They simply helped themselves to her money, used her to obtain drugs, and made her cook and clean for them. She wore second-hand glasses for almost forty years and was ashamed to tell anyone. She still has not told her children. Nadeline has been urged to tell her children so they would be aware of what she had experienced, allowing them to understand her better, but still she refuses to tell. When asked how she saw, she says she would use the lines and move them around on her face allowing her to see a little better!

Nadeline says she was forced to eat the same thing daily for dinner which was her only meal beyond black coffee, water and the occasional soda. This one meal a day consisted of a frozen chicken patty and a baked potato for almost 20 years. Nadeline says she was forced to cook for both Vissy and her alcoholic husband. She was not allowed to eat anything she prepared for the couple beyond what scraps she ingested while cooking. After cooking the couple's meals, she was forced to leave the kitchen and go back to her room while they ate.

She was forced to get up in the middle of the night during the husband's drunken tirades and cook for him just to avoid getting beaten. Vissy had family and friends coming and going on a regular basis. No one questioned the behaviour inside the home, just accepted this abuse as normal. Obviously, no one loved Nadeline nor did they care about Nadeline beyond her social security check.

Nadeline says she was accosted by Vissy's drunk husband multiple times; this was a stout factory worker in the prime of life and obviously much stronger than the 85-year-old woman. Nadeline says she was grabbed from behind and slammed to the floor by him when she did not make it to her room fast enough to suit him. She was routinely cursed, physically beaten in the form of slaps and hits on the head and across the face. She was mentally and emotionally abused by both Vissy and her drunk husband almost daily; telling her she was worthless, yelling she could not do anything right, and telling her the obvious, "nobody loves or cares about you." This forced her self-worth lower than ever imagined.

She says she was mocked as the family pet when the couple had guests. She was made to clean the house on a routine basis and clean up after the couple regularly. She would be locked in her room if the couple was leaving for any extended period. She would be locked in her room if the couple was having guests over that were not aware she lived in the home. She says she was hidden from non-family friends and any surprise visitors.

She was able to regain a sense of freedom and self-worth after a year or so on her own. With the help of her children, she was able to regain control of her finances. She found an affordable senior apartment and started making new friends. She was forced to pay the bills that Vissy had ran up in her name. She says she no longer lives in fear. She enjoys her bathtub, shower, and laundry facilities as if they are prize possessions instead of everyday essentials.

She has gained weight as she enjoys going out to eat, picking her own groceries, and cooking meals for herself. She has been able to maintain a somewhat distant and strained at times, relationship with her three middle-aged children who were virtual strangers until a few years ago. Although she has started to thrive on her own, Nadeline continues to hide the living situation she was forced into by Vissy from her children. She keeps silent about the abuse, using a bucket to bath and toilet and being physically abused by Vissy's drunken husband in the middle of the night.

Chapter 3
The Mayor Egg Yolk

"Oh, but I'm the mayor," he cried. "I can do anything I want! I can keep one of the busiest roadways blocked until my wife opens her wine bar; yes, I can, yes, I can," he screams jumping up and down as if he is a six-year-old child having a temper tantrum.

A local post-office conversation exposes the frustration, unhappiness, and misuse of power by the local mayor. 14th Street, New Castle, Indiana remained closed for years with the intention to stay this way at the ignorance of the decision-makers on this subject. This street divides the town of New Castle, Indiana and runs directly in front of the post office, older part of uptown, and allows access from the north to south or vice versa parts of town.

With the city's new-found love of grants, they intended originally to place higher-end apartments and restaurants uptown to revive the downtown area. Well, this revitalisation did not happen. Instead, the only building that was refurbished is now designated as HUD (housing and urban development) apartments where rent is guaranteed by and from the government who paid to refurbish this building in the first place (minus what was rumoured to have been pocketed).

Furthermore, this street remained inaccessible to everyone in town until this mayor and his wife decided a wine bar would benefit them. Lo and behold, the opening of the new wine bar brought the opening of 14th Street. The uptown area of New Castle remains a ghost town and run down despite the funding that was supposed to have brought an upgrade and a multitude of new business!

Mr Mayor's decisions are hideous; downtown is dead, drugs are at an all-time high, corruption is everywhere starting from the top as now the board has determined there is "misappropriation of funds". The mayor thrives, personally buying up everything in town while the city itself is in debt and floundering. Are the words theft and misappropriation being misused? His own street commissioner was arrested for stalking and had six types of drugs in his pockets, was wasted on pills, and arrested while attending a town board meeting! Exactly how many decisions were made under the influence of drugs? Sad to say we will never know but we can look around and see! As for his residence, it is rumoured the mayor maintains a local residence on S 11th Street New Castle, Indiana and resides regularly at an out-of-town address; corruption to gain and maintain political office!

The unbeloved mayor of New Castle, Indiana, takes credit for projects far beyond his reach. He benefits himself and his cohorts, not the public, and treats city employees rather poorly when asked. He is rumoured to make decisions on his personal preferences not the preferences of the entire community. It has been rumoured Mr Egg Yolk is trying to relive his childhood and bring back the past as noted with his project selections such as dances at the local armoury. Nostalgia for a second or two is good for releasing feel-good endorphins but to live in the past is dangerous, non-productive, and costly both in time and money.

Mr Egg Yolk allows the local first responders to act in a very non-professional and dangerous manner as in the case of using their red flashing lights to get to lunch on time. How do you take an emergency vehicle seriously when you watch them race down the highway with their lights on and you yield to this thinking it is an emergency in which someone is harmed or in need of emergent treatment, only to meet up with them five minutes later in line at the local McDonald's! Absolutely disgraceful behaviour. This is stupidity at its best and a testament to the type of unprofessional, neglectful, and blatant misuse of power there is in New Castle, Indiana.

Each person who witnesses this childish behaviour now has the inclination to avoid the emergency lights due to the inappropriate conduct and use of power of these obviously immature and overrated individuals who choose to act like children playing with a toy. So, when they are avoided on the highway with their lights on and residents refuse to yield, they only have themselves to blame. They are not saving lives, they are acting as if it doesn't matter and placing innocent lives and individuals in need of help in danger! This is not professional in any sense of the word. This is creating a very dangerous environment and to believe you will never be on the receiving end, is quite foolish in thought as people are watching and will make decisions on what they see and experience. It has become so bad that the city has posted signs saying yield to emergency vehicles!

Each of us has two personas, the private and the public. These individuals are exhibiting their lack of respect for the public and their position by allowing their hedonistic side to

33

be exhibited in a very public fashion. New Castle Indiana, let's have an ambulance race down the highway for a Big Mac – really, truly disgraceful behaviour. You are saying in one aspect, city of New Castle residents piss on you, you mean nothing, and your life is worth nothing, I don't take this position seriously, and you should not take me seriously in any situation! Message received loud and clear – no respect for the local mayor, no respect for the residents, loss of control throughout the entire city that is gradually wasting away.

One family even goes as far as to say Mr Egg Yolk burned his own property to avoid taking it back or cleaning it up! Apparently, Mayor Yolk sold a local home he had to a young New Castle couple with two children. The couple agreed to the purchase price, paid the down payment and signed the contract. After 3 years, they were in over their head. They were not able to keep up with repairs, taxes and general maintenance due to finances and health. They decided to forfeit their down payment and give Mr Yolk the house back. This couple, the Guppies, were to meet Mr Yolk at a specific time and place; they recall it as the local Hardee's restaurant at 4pm. Mr Yolk did not show up for the meeting; instead, the couple find out the following day that the house had burned to the ground the same night. This house had no electricity, no water and no gas. Basically, an empty home with absolutely no natural or environmental factors to start a flame. Should it be Egg Yolk arsonist instead of mayor? Recently the local city garage housing city vehicles and equipment burned; it is reported/rumoured that Mr Yolk was there removing things from the ashes and moving things around in the burned rubble – inappropriate to tamper with evidence of a potential arson. Again, should it be arsonist instead of mayor?

New Castle, IN has a history of its mayors burning their property for profit as with Mayor Bug Aires who is rumoured to have burned his family's grocery store several times to collect insurance money while still in office in the 1980s. Elected officials get elected with very little turn out of voting citizens in the New Castle, Henry County, Indiana area. This happens with most local and county offices in the area. It is hard to believe that 2,500 of the 15,000 or less residents who reside in New Castle, Henry County, IN, elect those who are supposed to run things, but it happens. Lack of interest, complacency or ignorant bliss might be the reason; we will never know but we will reap the havoc!

Chapter 4
The Unexpected
Unwanted Visitor

Imagine someone walking into your home and having a seat in your living room with you. You do not know this person who just graced your entrance, he is a total stranger and unbeknownst to you, a wanted murderer in a nearby city.

Mr and Mrs Foggle are a kindly elderly couple who sit engrossed in their early evening television selections in the den toward the back of their home. They both hear noises coming from the front of the house that sounded as if someone had opened the screen door and was in the kitchen starting to cook. What they hear is pots and pans being moved around. They live alone and do not have company at the time, so this is both strange and concerning for the couple.

Mr Foggle starts to stand and turns his head toward the kitchen when he is eye to eye with the intruder. This stranger is a very large man of six feet or more and weighs what Mr Foggle guesses to be at least 300 pounds. The intruder who appears unkept is wearing wrinkled jeans and a muddy white hooded sweatshirt that is open in the front displaying a red spatter-stained white T-shirt. This trespasser has a full, shabby, dark-coloured beard and abnormally large bloodshot eyes. Mr Foggle can't help but notice that the intruder seems to have very large dilated pupils hiding any colour and leaving nothing but black that matches the large bruise under his left eye. His nose appears very wide and looks as if it has been bleeding with dried black crust along the edges. His ruddy skin is glistening with perspiration and a toboggan covers dark curly hair that is peeking out the sides.

Mr Foggle continues to walk towards this man who he has never seen before and who has so brazenly invaded his home and ransacked his kitchen, apparently searching for something or anything. Mr Foggle starts shouting, "Who are you and what do you want?!" all the while pointing towards the front door for this unwanted visitor to exit the home.

Mrs Foggle has now gotten off the sofa and started to walk up behind her husband. She notices the reflection and realises this stranger has a gun in his left hand and blood along the sleeve of his sweatshirt. She instinctively yells to her husband; he has a gun, I'm calling the police. The stranger then pulls the gun from beside his body to a raised position and points it at Mr Foggle, telling his wife to sit down and shut up! Mrs Foggle does just that and goes back to the sofa from where she came. Unbeknownst to the intruder, she maintains possession of her cell phone in the pocket of her sweater. Once she has regained her composure, she ever so slightly slips her hand in her pocket finding the ringer button on her phone and turns it off; she then latches on to her Kleenex pulling it out of her pocket and dabs the tears from her eyes.

The intruder is now face to face with Mr Foggle and shoves the gun into his stomach telling him to move into the hallway leading away from the den. All the while he is asking Mr Foggle if there is any money in the house, what kind of pills do you take, how much money do you have, where is your wife's purse, have you got any booze here and then says give me your wallet. Mr Foggle readily hands over his wallet, tells him he lives on social security and there is no money in the house as they have a hard time just making ends meet from month to month. The intruder then directs Mr Foggle to find his wife's purse after he had rummaged in the wallet finding nothing and impulsively tossing it beside him allowing the contents to spill out over the floor.

They have made their way back into the den where Mrs Foggle is quietly sitting in the same spot at the end of the sofa looking out over the backyard. "Where is your purse?" asks Mr Foggle and she replies; under the head of the bed where it always is! The intruder then pokes the gun again in the ribs of Mr Foggle, forcing him back out of the room and down the hall to the bedroom. Mr Foggle is puzzled as his wife keeps her purse on the floor of the closet in the entryway to their home. They make their way through the bedroom door and the scraping of the door on the hardwood floor startles the intruder, who in turn pushes Mr Foggle forward, causing him to trip and fall on the floor at the foot of the bed. As he is lying there puzzled as to what happened, the intruder is yelling; get the purse, get the damn purse, and stand up.

Mrs Foggle is no longer in the den but headed toward the front door as soon as she heard the bedroom door at the back of the house start to creak open. She is now outside and sees the car not 10 feet away in the drive and no one else around. She goes to the far side of the car and gently opens the door and gets in the back seat. She crouches in the floor of the car hidden and she calls 911. She reports an intruder in her home and urges them to please come right away as this burglar is holding a gun to her husband and has blood all over his clothes.

Mr Foggle and the intruder are now back in the den and the intruder is yelling; where is your purse, you damn lying woman, there was no purse under the bed. The intruder again starts to swear as they step forward toward the sofa finding Mrs Foggle gone. Mr Foggle with his wife now out of harm's way, starts to taunt the man; she's gone, she went for the police, she's telling them everything.

Shut up; yells the intruder, visually flushed and perspiring profusely again.

Mr Foggle keeps going; I hear the sirens, do you hear them, she called the police! she's outsmarted you, didn't she. Mr Foggle goes on; you won't be getting her purse now, I'll bet she took it with her when she ran out the front door!

Now the intruder is visibly upset and yelling; move, damn it – move," and pushes Mr Foggle back out of the den down the hallway towards the front door. Mr Foggle starts to step faster and faster as he can hear the roar of sirens coming from the outside. He shoves open the front screen and steps to the side on his porch as the intruder bursts through the front door and keeps on going, out through the front yard and down the sidewalk just as the police pull up. He starts to run, and they instinctively start to run after him yelling; Stop, hold it right there, don't move!

Mrs Foggle pops her head up just enough to see the police and then gets out of the car, running toward the front porch and her husband yelling; are you ok, are you ok?!

I was so scared; she says. She is now on the porch standing beside her husband with her arms around his waist. Again she asks; did he hurt you, are you ok?

Mr Foggle being the man's man that he prides himself to be, says, "Yes, of course I am OK; didn't you see him run away?"

As they stand there holding each other on the front porch, the front yard, and sidewalk start to fill with emergency vehicles, police and bystanders looking on. An officer walks toward the couple asking if they are hurt; when they reply no, he tells them; you're lucky, this man is wanted for a brutal murder that happened yesterday in Muncie" (a town not 20 minutes away).

The officer continues to tell them this intruder was involved in a similar incident trying to rob an elderly couple and shot them both multiple times, killing the couple and then he proceeded to cut them both into pieces. The officer continues telling the Foggles this man has a history of multiple arrests and past imprisonment for violence and drugs. Officers walk the intruder back towards the house; they place the intruder who is now in handcuffs, in the back of a running patrol car and speed away. The Foggles are left looking on in disbelief.

Chapter 5
Injustice for All

Don't arrest him, he's the sheriff's son!

How does one sheriff's son take pot to school in his father's (the former sheriff's) truck and get caught by a drug sniffing K-9 of the local sheriff's department who are making the rounds meant to keep drugs out of schools, and the local deputies finding this marijuana refuse to arrest the son of their former boss? Insane prejudicial behaviour, truly biased behaviour on the part of the K-9 deputy, and unconstitutional to the law and the public. Sheriff Barker can go into the court system and get it all swept under the rug as part of the "good ole boy" club in the corrupt town of New Castle, Indiana. Hence, injustice; you and I go to jail – no free pass for far less than drugs!

Meanwhile, another young man (a neighbouring county sheriff's son, not much older than the Barker boy) is pulled over for drunk driving and readily arrested and placed in the local Henry County jail. A jail that is known to be offender friendly by allowing drugs to pass through their doors and into the cells. This child was beaten to death – literally beaten to death – by multiple inmates inside a county jail for possession of his cell phone and left to die by the healthcare providers of the jail. It was told to me/rumoured, initially the beatings started by the deputies and assisting arresting Sherriff. This young boy, barely 20 years of age, was then taken to the local hospital for assessment after the first rumoured beating took place then on to jail.

This young man was then taken to the jail and housed first with the child molesters who are supposed to be less violent and beaten again for the second time. He was then moved again to the more violent young population of prisoners who have nothing to lose and everything to prove as a life-time criminal. A drunken 20-year-old kid with absolutely no record was placed among seasoned criminals with a gang name attached to them. These are hoodlums and repeat offenders who lack respect, integrity and a sense of moral normality that have no chance at a normal life outside of prison. This boy was again beaten for the third time. This time beaten to death, allowed to be left lying on a cell floor for three days without medical attention. The person sharing this with me says his son is in jail at this time for murder, nonetheless, and describes his murdering son's current situation as "living fat as can be smoking his e-cigarette." Living fat to me indicates a good situation, not a punishing situation. Go to jail to lay around and watch television and smoke is not punishment, it's rent-free housing with taxpayers paying the utility bills!

Consequently, one of the prisoners who committed this violent, vicious and senseless act of murder was overheard on jail surveillance saying to his girlfriend; you would not believe what I had to do to get this phone and call you. Now this repeat criminal, Justice Faggen, is facing murder charges and was given only six years for his crimes prior to and his in-house jail murder involvement!

To add insult to injury and enlighten folks as to the type of treatment and behaviour that goes on inside the Henry County Jail, this young man, now beaten three different times, was placed in solitary confinement and supposed to have been monitored by the health care professionals inside the jail. He was ignored for several days and ultimately lost his life to abuse, negligence and blatant ignorance by those in charge who swear to serve, protect and do no harm. This young man, also the son of a sheriff and more like me and you on the outside of the good old boy network that operates in the judicial system of Henry County, Indiana, lost his life as the result of being beaten to death and ignored while in police custody at the Henry County Jail. That is frightening business.

Maleficence dictates do no harm, justice dictates follow the rule of law and uphold the constitution and position you are in, prejudice and ignorance dictate the behaviour of the Henry County Sherriff's Department and the local jail employees.

Still another young man participates in a harmless prank of toilet papering trees at a home of someone who steadily harassed him throughout his high school days. This young man is easily arrested for his senior prank and readily placed on probation and doing community service – *toilet paper verses marijuana!* The clear winner is the injustice, the obstruction of the law, and the good ole boy network that is above the law. The same laws we taxpayers in the community are expected to follow.

Hey, judge, what are you thinking, or are you not thinking at all? Slapping your friend on the back while the rest of us suffer the consequences of your lack of self-control and personal respect for the community you are to represent 100%

of, not just your friends. One young man dies at the hands of the local officials, one young man suffers post-traumatic stress due to the actions of the local authorities, while the child of the former sheriff who has illegal drugs in his possession, at a school no less, is unscathed and continues to misbehave!

As recent as November 2018, a trustee (inmate with special privileges) of the Henry County Jail overdosed on Fentanyl; if the officials of the Henry County Jail were doing their job, this would not be possible! So, what is this type of behaviour attributed to? According to the fellow whose son is "living fat as can be smoking his e-cigarette", seems to think "dirty cops bringing it in"; this would make sense as they are the authority and the ones with access. Poor judgment, greed, lack of self-control and ignorance can also be said to play a role in this if you asked me! I wonder what Deputy Chief David in charge of the jail is up to, what his drug screen would look like, what he is buying and selling, and exactly how much he is profiting off his drug dealing in the jail.

As recent as the summer of 2018, an inmate of work release, Sally Wilkins, ran away and was rumoured to be gone for months. These incidents of overdose leading to death on Fentanyl and the runaway prisoner were never printed in the local paper. Was it due to intentional cover-up of incompetence within the sheriff's department? Would make sense if you think back to the refusal of the sheriff's department to give a copy of the death report of Curtis Wagner to his older brother Ronnie. What else is being hidden and why?

Yet again, I hear another story from a mother who says her son was beaten at the local jail during an arrest and while having a seizure. She tells me that 14 years ago in New Castle,

Indiana, her son hit a stop sign soon after he started driving and was not as compliant as he should have been during the arrest. This teenager at the time had been beaten by the local police/sheriff's deputies who were grown men! How could you justify beating a human having a seizure? This mother says when her son was handcuffed during this arrest, he started seizing and the local police and sheriff's deputies who arrested him started beating him once again. His injuries included two broken wrists, two broken ankles, 103 contusions, and he was hospitalised for several weeks.

Over the course of the next three days, he experienced 13 more convulsive events. She tells me she went to the court system to file a complaint and was told by the then police chief Barker that if she made a scene, rallied on the courthouse lawn with a gay activist group, or pursued any action against the Henry County Police or Sheriff's Departments, her house would be burned to the ground and there would be nothing remaining of her, her son, her husband or her business – a local breakfast restaurant that was a corner staple for 30 years in New Castle, Indiana. She goes on to tell me Mr Barker, the police chief or sheriff at the time, told her she would "be harassed and ran out of town." Fear for herself and her family caused her to place this on the back burner of her life, but clearly it has left its mark on her.

I believe these things are truer than not. As I said before, I myself was harassed with one traffic ticket after another to the tune of 91 traffic points in less than a year and frightened by the local police and sheriff's departments, even placed in jail for a week. Seven days in jail with a cell full of women who were there for murder, drugs, theft and other assorted crimes.

I slept on the floor in front of the cell by the door, the light above my head was never out, the mat I had to sleep on was old, worn, smelled and was approximately ¼" thick, so in essence, I spent a week sleeping on a cement floor, no pillow, and a blanket so worn and thin, it had more holes than Swiss cheese. Me, who never committed any crime beyond drive my car. I was exposed to more drugs in the Henry County Jail than on the street. I was actually told "I am harassing you" by Deputy Chief Jay Davis of the sheriff's department.

As inmates go out for work release, they bring drugs back in, tucked in their vagina or rectum. These drugs are passed through the cell walls from one inmate to another. Drugs are also smuggled in by the weekend offenders; obviously someone is not proficient at their job or this would not happen. How in the hell do they not smell pot in the fucking jail, that is so very, very, very small?! They don't want to! I personally wonder exactly how much money Deputy Chief David makes off his inside jail drug hustle, obviously enough to not care about the consequences of his actions.

Those in charge of the jail are known to have sexual relationships with prisoners, to the point of bearing children who go on to become wards of the state as jail employees, will not admit to guilt and sex with a prisoner, and prisoners who are there for murder and other assorted crimes are convicted and could care less about children conceived while in jail. As in the case of Major Nick MiKork. In this situation, the mother of his jail house affair was there for murdering an elderly female who lived alone and was very frail. You could say he is just as guilty of beating to death this elderly female as was the prisoner. These are only a few of the known things that have happened; can you imagine what we don't know!

I witnessed the murderer of Jeff Wistfield who was in the cell to the left of me and an inmate in my cell perversely exploit themselves in an attempt to have sex between the cell walls; first she watches him do himself and then she does herself while sitting on the concrete table (you are supposed to eat off of), allowing him to watch between the crack in the wall! Keep in mind, I have never ever been exposed to anything such as this. I do not watch or partake in pornography of any type, did not raise my child to swear, was not raised in a home with any such vile behaviour, and must witness it because of police ignorance! It could easily be said this is post-traumatic stress that they have caused me to deal with daily! The local sheriff's department also allowed someone to pull a knife on me while I was walking my dogs, something I did daily and have for the past 9 years in a cemetery close to my home. The sheriff's deputy who acted like he might be 12 years old, did absolutely nothing about it despite my complaints; this is promoting violence – a knife is a deadly weapon! The man who attempted to stab me was very angry, six feet, and 300 or so pounds, pointing and lunging forward, knife in hand, I repeat, lunging violently toward me and my 10-pound dogs! Nothing was done because he called his friend Moore of the sheriff's department, who had it swept under the rug. If they will participate in coitus with inmates, it should not be a surprise to me nothing was done about this violent incident. For me this incident was the last I am going to tolerate and spawned my desire to write this book and expose these people!

Later I learned a woman in my cell did in fact commit the crime, accomplice to murder, that she was exonerated from. Years after she was released, and, in another setting, she told me the story of Mr Wistfield's death and that she was the getaway driver. She knew the murderer had a gun because he had shown it to her and others earlier in the evening while at a party with friends (Note: her small children were in another room.) She heard the gunshots while waiting for her friend to come back to the car and after he got in, they simply drove away, essentially getting away with murder!

Chapter 6

Oh My God, He Just Shot My Mother – Now He Is Pointing at Me

It was just like any other Sunday morning in the middle of November for the family of Blake Winfred. They had just arrived home after a nice lunch at the family's favourite Sunday after-church restaurant, the Stone House Diner. This Sunday November 16th was as normal as any other Sunday for the 15-year-old Blake who lived with his mother and stepfather of several years. Blake had eaten his usual chicken fried steak meal with his parents getting their normal pot roast and potato lunch special; the entire family eating every morsel they were served, as they always did on their way home from church.

Blake walked in the house first, he was a few steps ahead of his parents, he recalls hanging up his coat and going to his bedroom for a nap as usual on Sunday afternoon in the winter months. Blake recalls the conversation as ordinary during lunch; his parents talking about the upcoming holidays and the Thanksgiving meal they would serve to friends and family that always came over this time of year to celebrate and be

49

close together, giving thanks for one another. Blake says his parents were holding hands as they normally do during church service and he recalls the time at home before the church service as rushed to get out the door once everyone was fed, dressed and ready to go. All this; he begins to weep as he is talking; was normal for a Sunday at my house.

Blake recalls resting on his bed in his cosy and quiet bedroom tucked under the back staircase. The shades drawn to almost blacken the room with a few inches of grey light peeking through the bottom portion of his window. Blake says he started hearing loud voices – his mother was yelling, almost screaming, but he could not make out the words she was saying. Again, the tears are running from his eyes down his pink flushed cheeks and he goes on to say that he was frightened by the noise as his mother rarely raised her voice. Blake remained lying on his back on his bed listening as the voices and yelling got steadily louder and angrier. Now it is not just his mother, it is his stepfather also yelling back at her in an obviously heated exchange. He decides to go into the living room and check on his parents as he is unnerved by the abnormal commotion he is hearing.

Blake opens the door gently as to not raise awareness of himself as he is steadily getting more and more frightened by what he is hearing. He makes his way through the living room, into the kitchen and stands frozen just inside the kitchen door. He eyes two coffee cups still sitting at opposite ends of the table. His mother's purse spilled out on the floor beside the kitchen counter directly under the sink. The water is still running, the teapot on the stove is steaming and whistling without notice of anyone in the room. Blake hears his mother scream, stop, and he quickly glances toward the voice coming from around the corner. A few years after purchasing the house, the family turned the former breakfast nook into a mud room that leads into the kitchen from outside the house.

He sees his mother laying face up against the back door, blood draining from every orifice of her face and several bloody spots on her chest; everything is a blur, he says. she had one arm in her coat and one out; she looked scared to death. Her eyes were wide open, her pupils were huge and seemingly fixed on something like she was staring ahead at me. She wasn't moving except when the bullets hit her body, causing violent jerking. She was no longer screaming; she was lifeless sprawled out on the floor.

Blake remembers seeing his stepfather standing over his mother's bloody lifeless body at the doorway that exits the kitchen with a gun in his right hand. Blake says he wasn't aware his stepfather even had a gun and never dreamed he would use one to kill or harm his mother. Blake recalls his stepfather continuing to point and shoot his mother's lifeless body, each bullet causing her body to jerk and spew blood. She was a crumpled bloody mess on the floor; her efforts to escape him were hopeless, yet he kept shooting at her.

Blake says he was now screaming; mom!!! and gasping for air as he started to move closer to his mother and suddenly his chest felt heavy and burning. He starts to run closer and closer to his mother lying dead on the floor. His stepfather has now turned toward him looking him in the eye, no tears, no frowning, no sadness, his face is just flushed red and perspiring. Blake says he had never seen the man looking at him before, as this man was eyeing him with disgust and anger on his face, and then raised his right hand and started shooting at him again. Hitting him in the abdomen, again in the chest-hence the burning sensation he felt before – he must have thought the initial shot killed him – and finally the neck. Blake falls to the floor, able to see blood pooling around his head as he sees his stepfather leap over him and exit the kitchen, not saying a word, just leaving.

He loses consciousness, only to awaken three days later in the intensive care unit of a local trauma hospital. Blake finds his mother has already been buried by his family who did not know if he would survive the ordeal or not. He says he can see nothing but flashbacks of his mother lying on the floor jerking with spouts of blood coming from her limp lifeless body. He hears the hum of the machines around him, the beeps, alarms and other hospital noises, but cannot say anything because he is hooked to mechanical ventilation. He can only squeeze the hand of his father who is sitting beside him, slumped over the bed, holding his hand.

Once awake and recovering enough to breathe on his own without ventilation, he starts to speak and remember bits and pieces of what happened, all the while having the picture of his mother's bloody and lifeless body haunting the back of his mind and crowding his thoughts. Blake starts to question his father, who has remained at his bedside holding his hand for weeks, as to what happened and suddenly starts to sob uncontrollably remembering his mother lifeless at the back door.

An alarm sounds on his heart monitor and he jumps in fear as he cannot control his weeping. His father begins to pat his hand and try to comfort and calm him by softly saying his name and telling him; it will be OK, you're OK, you will be OK, you're not going to die. After several months of hospitalisation, psychiatry and physical therapy, Blake went home with his father to try and continue his recovery, picking up the pieces of his life as a teenager. All the while trying to deal with and reliving the brutal death of his mother on a day-to-day basis.

Blake recalls the trial as cruel, having to listen to his stepfather make excuses for why he shot and killed his mother. Admitting such petty arguments as she was smothering him. She was making him lose money, she was holding him back, she was aging him with a stepson he did not want and was tired of pretending he cared about.

His stepfather remarked; I did not want her anymore, but I wasn't letting her go either! She wanted to leave! I told her get out and then when she turned to put her coat on, I shot her in the back first just to see what would happen. I wanted her to suffer just like she made me suffer all these years. When she turned around and started screaming stop, she was crying and hysterical; I kept on shooting. It made me feel good!

Blake recalls this man as having no remorse, and spoke of his mother as he would a stray animal, and all the while smiling as if he was pleased by what he had done. He said he rid himself of a couple of pests; he stood and said this right in the middle of the court proceedings!

Blake remembers his father holding his arm trying to comfort him as he broke down weeping into his hands. His father yelled psychopath. There were loud gasps, lots of talking and noise during the court uproar that happened after he said he rid himself of a couple of pests. Everyone was made to leave the courtroom shortly after the judge got everybody quiet again as there was nothing left to say.

Chapter 7

She's Sleeping with Our Children

Now elderly, this father is totally distraught as he shares his wife's secret that included sex with their sons. She shared her drug loot with their sons. She trained their sons to steal, lie and participate in other acts of deviance for her own hedonistic pleasure, he says between sobs. She is seemingly meek and quiet upon first introduction, but as it turns out, she is really a child molesting devil who participated in sex with our two boys. Now they repeatedly taunt me in my sleep. I am their father and her former husband, them telling "me to disturbing" mom says we are much better equipped sexually than you are has become overwhelmingly disturbing!"

Mr Loston is sobbing, his hands are shaking, and he can hardly get his words out as he begins to explain why he is so upset today. Normally Mr Loston is subdued himself, not venturing into his private and personal life, just his medical issues and the reasons he has set an appointment. Today is different, he is obviously shaken and distraught because his normally well-groomed self has given way to being dishevelled. His wrinkled clothes, his unkept hair, and growth of an uncharacteristic beard are evident his personal hygiene and appearance are taking the backseat to something.

He is speaking louder than normal between sobs. "You will not believe this!" he says. He continues, "I can't keep it in any longer, it's driving me crazy. I just passed her in the hallway, she must be a patient also," he says. My ex-wife, Betty, that just left, was sexually active with my boys and was in fact their first lover. This happened when they were kids about 10 and 11 years old.

I married her while we were both young and she lived with her sister because she had no other choice, her parents had been killed in a plane crash several years ago. I knew she was orphaned and had been passed from one family member to another as a child, each more impoverished than the one before. I had no idea she possessed such a dark and deviant nature about her; he says. Mr Loston continues, and I sit across the room and listen, as he obviously needs to vent and wants to be heard.

I remember when we met; he says; Betty was young and a pretty girl too. She seemed so delicate and shy. She was quiet when we went out the first time, never saying much. Bet, that's what I called her, my Bet – it was an inside joke. I would tell her she was the best bet I had ever made. Anyway, that first night, Bet let me order her dinner and had even trembled when our hands accidently touched as I opened the car door for her that first evening.

I was around 45 and Betty was only 30 or so at the time; he says, no longer sobbing but half-heartedly smiling. I thought I was so lucky finding such a nice girl in such a rough place; he goes on to say. I had no idea what she was really like until much later when the new had worn off and the real Betty started showing up. My friends and family tried to warn me; he says; but I didn't listen and believed everything she said.

Everything from the first lie that I was her first real grown-up date and relationship because she had not dated since she was 15 and in high school. She told me she accompanied a senior to his prom!

I was blinded by her and her lies. I think I loved her so much I would have believed anything. She said I was an old fool. I believed I was so fortunate with this pretty young girl 15 years my junior giving me all this attention. Oh, and I was pleased! All my friends were envious; he says. Hell, they were dating middle-aged, overweight, divorced women who had half-grown kids and me with this young girl. I was on cloud nine!

Those first years were good. She was soft and consoling, wanted to please, and seemed to fall into the role of girlfriend with little left to be desired. Betty would cook meals and invite me over to her sister's for dinner and family time, as she called it. She would send me love letters and I would send them back; it was heaven for the gruff middle-aged man that I was. I would find flowers on my windshield and notes in my door. I was smitten quick, swept off my feet by this sweet young lady I thought I had found.

So, after those first two years and no disagreements, I felt it would be a good idea to propose, and I did. She seemed just perfect for a life-time partner, wife and mother for the children I desperately wanted at my age, now 47 and starting to grey. She said yes; it was a simple but lovely proposal. I planned a nice quiet picnic in the local park. We sat along the bank of the rushing river listening to the water. The smell of freshness in the spring air seemed to engulf us and keep out every other distraction – it was perfect.

There was an April nip lingering in the air and the slightest hint of spring flowers dotting the green landscape around us. I was so happy; he says. I had bought her a ring with the help of her sister who told me the size that would most likely fit; I wanted her to put it on and never take it off. It was from me to her; she was going to be my wife and partner. That ring solidified my feelings of hope, happiness and a future. Now looking back, I think the sister plotted to get this conniving girl out of her own home…; and he starts to frown again.

After several years, we got pregnant. Betty gave birth to my first son, Elvin, named after my father. The following year we had Eric, a second son and obviously her favourite. Betty would dote on Eric shamelessly even with Elvin in the room. Elvin tried desperately to get her attention, approval and love. Her partiality was evident to only me at first, I thought, as she would not behave this way if we were out shopping or visiting friends and relatives.

Later, as Eric started getting bigger, it became obvious to everyone something wasn't right. Each time we went out, she would question where Eric was. She would keep him on her lap all the time. She wouldn't allow him to play with the other children, not even his brother. Finally, after months of this odd behaviour, keeping him close to her all the time, she began to stoke him in very unnatural and unnerving ways that caused our friends and family to finally speak up.

She's treating him just like Abe, her sister told me.

Who is Abe? I asked.

Abe turned out to be the child his wife Betty had at age 15 with her prom date. This child was killed in a fire when he was 12 years old, just three years before Betty and I started to date. Abe was spending the night with his uncle who consequently was an alcoholic and drug abuser. This uncle lived in a nearby town in a hotel apartment he could rent by the week, as he had difficulty keeping a job for any extended period. The apartment they were in caught fire; I have no idea how or why he says. Instead of trying to get out and get Abe out, the uncle ran and hid in the bathtub. He turned the water on himself, lay in the bathtub in the pooling water and left it running to avoid being burned. He left Abe alone in the living room to be consumed by the fire, ultimately burning to his death. The uncle suffered smoke inhalation issues and minor burns but survived.

Oh my God!; I exclaim because I am stunned by this admission. He says he questioned his sister-in-law asking her why she didn't tell him this long ago. He says she only shook her lowered head and said I don't know!

He says his sister-in-law, Becky, told him that before Abe died Betty would allow him to drink alcohol, party as in do drugs with her, and sleep with her in an incestual fashion. Betty is treating Eric just like she did Abe; she used to stroke him in the very same way, arousing him just like she does Eric.

She doesn't think of this as inappropriate and I am unsure why; he says. I think it might be due to alcohol and drugs, due to herself being raped as a child, or another psychosis. I just don't know what she is thinking; he says and hangs his head again and allows the tears to flow.

As friends and family notice and continue to mention the inappropriateness of Betty's behaviour, I pay more attention myself as well. She had started allowing him in the bath with her, letting him give her a sponge bath, touch her breasts and fondle them openly while I am in and out of the bathroom. Once while shaving, I witnessed them in the mirror.

She stood up in the tub allowing him to touch her vaginal area. She was moaning loudly as he reached up to grab her and stroke between her legs. I yell stop and whirl around to look directly at them. That's not right and certainly not normal; I say. They laughed together and dismissed me, saying we do it all the time. I am stunned and can only turn and walk away.

As I compose myself; he says; I step back into the bathroom where they remain, my wife and my son. Now she has her left leg upon the side of the tub, and he is on his knees with his face very near her vaginal area. She has one hand on his head, guiding him toward her moaning all the while telling him it is your turn next. As she presses his face into her vaginal area, I can see him stroke her vagina with his tongue and she moans even louder, purring and saying; hit the high spot just like I taught you.

I am appalled and start to cry as I watch my wife and son; he is grasping her behind and obviously getting more aroused by the moment. He is so forceful, she loses her balance and starts to fall back against the wall of the tub, they are both flush-faced and start to laugh. They begin to fondle each other all over again. His hands are on her breasts and her hands are grasping his penis. I can hardly believe what I am seeing; he says. She tells him sit on the side of the tub, it's your turn. They remain very unaware of me in the doorway watching or they blatantly just don't care.

She has him sitting on the side of the tub now and starts to run her hands up his legs, ever inching closer to him blowing on his penis with her pursed lips. He is becoming more and more aroused as she finally reaches him with her mouth and takes him in. He lets out a very loud and unmistakable moan and grabs her hair in his hands, pulling her face closer into his groin, moving with her at a hungered pace. She braces his buttock in one of her hands and places the other over his scrotum and begins to massage him gently as his penis remains tight in her mouth.

The rhythm of watching my wife make love to my son is making me sick and I lean forward and wretch. They pay no mind to me and she maintains her position, looking at me with only her eyes. He is leaning forward now, jutted towards her. She allows his penis to withdraw from her mouth that is full of his semen and starts kissing him all over his groin area. First his limp penis, then his balls get a thorough kissing and licking by my wife who is smiling and staring at me. After she cleans him, in the same fashion a cat would clean a kitten by licking it, they sit back in the tub together, both flushed, exhausted and satisfied. I pack my clothes and leave as they remain in the bathroom."

When asked why he had not turned them in and tried to save his children from incest and molestation, he says he did and they both lied saying he was making it up.

She ultimately got custody of our sons and this behaviour remained throughout their childhood. Both boys remain in and out of jail, hooked on drugs and alcohol, and both in bad relationships. I believe this is because of the trauma they endured as children; he says. He continues no longer looking down or sobbing, but with a sad defeated look on his face.

"Eric said to me years later, Mom used to tell me I was better than you, my penis was bigger, and I was more of a man. This is not a normal healthy mother-son relationship by any stretch of the imagination, he says. "Shortly after, he asked me how old I was, me his father, when I had sex for the first time, and he tells me he was 10 and smiles at me! My recurring nightmare!"

Chapter 8

A Rifle, a Scope, a Murder Forgotten

Imagine walking into your local Casey's convenience store and finding a woman lying dead on the floor in a puddle of her own blood. She is stiff and blue, indicating she has been there a while. A single rifle shot through the clear glass in the dead of night hitting and killing its target while a small town was tucked into bed. In the dead of night, it would be easy to visualise your target in the bright white light of a convenience store that is all clear glass. Hidden across the street in the blackened woods with a silencer on your gun, you could also get away with it! There was a rumour or myth, as it is referred to by some, that Johnny Carson once said, "If you want to commit murder and get away with it, do it in New Castle, Indiana." The originator of this rumour is unknown but seemingly correct on more than one occasion.

Julie was fighting with her long-time husband who just happened to be a local police detective, Mr Stevie. He is known to be crooked, obsessive, terribly jealous and a bit narcissistic. People laugh that he was the only man they knew with stock in Clairol, as he was said to die his hair jet back weekly to avoid grey roots! Shortly after Julie was found shot to death at the local Casey's, Mr Stevie retired and left town.

Still today, Julie's killer has never been found or brought to justice.

Mr Stevie had a lot going for him that would allow him to get away with murder. The right access to his target. The right frame of mind after years of investigating this type of crime. In addition to the understanding that it would be hard to prove especially among his friends or himself who would be investigating this death. Motive, knowledge, and friends in all the right places is what people say allowed him to apparently get away with murder.

Mr Stevie had a reputation for using police and police vehicles to transport and sell drugs to support his lifestyle. A lifestyle that was not possible on a cop's salary. Buying expensive custom motorcycles, expensive cars and property. He is thought to be egotistical, narcissistic and an overall agitator to get his own way, whether it be right or wrong. A demanding over-cocky gentleman who prances about town afraid to bend over for fear of his hair falling out of place. He has a reputation for extreme violence and cannot be linked to solving any real crime. Mr Stevie is part of a long history of no-gooders (defined by me as those who corrupt for self-gratification by performing and promoting acts of hedonism, harm and greed) who have left New Castle, Henry County, IN extremely corrupt and full of crime run amuck.

Mr Stevie is much like the local judge. This judge frolics about town in a bowler hat and dull black umbrella as if he were walking down a rainy London avenue after dark in a Hitchcock film. Much like the judge with his concubine of supported females who seem to break any law including drunk driving, not paying child support and solicitation, Mr Stevie protects his female friends. These women are kept in local apartments for his own pleasure and if they put out, they avoid punishment for any action or law they defile. So, it's easy to see with individuals like these two at the helm, nothing will be done! I wonder if Johnny Carson ever met this judge.

Julie was rumoured to have told a friend a few days before her murder that Mr Stevie had shaken her violently, not allowing her to exit the front door of the home they shared and then slamming her face first into the tiled floor of the entryway. She is describing another drunken fight between the two, her face swollen, discoloured areas of black and blue scattered all over her forehead and cheeks, and pooled blood sits below her lower eye lids, forming two perfectly round black eyes.

The friend recalls; I cannot remember the last time I saw her without a black eye! She is rumoured to have said he always feels the need to pronounce he is the law and he will lay down the punishment as he is screaming and hitting me. Her friend says she told of him jerking her backward by her hair and winding her long dark hair around his right hand and punching her over and over in the face with his left hand. Not stopping the punishment until she was a crumpled pile on the floor; she is never sure if it was her collapse or his exhaustion that made him stop.

She tells her friend she hates him. After each beating, he stands before her, straightening himself and his clothes, telling her look what you made me do. He runs his hands through his meticulously groomed over-sprayed hair, waiting for her to remark. He always blames her for whatever has happed. He never fails to curse, belittle, and degrade her before he storms out of the room as if nothing happened.

Julie is not a beautiful woman; the victim was of a normally attractive appearance. She was approximately 5' something, more on the shorter side. She was not thin, not fat. She had medium length dark brown hair that fell at her shoulder and olive skin. In town, the victim can be recognised or identified with her job as the lady from the local CVS pharmacy for years. In addition to this, at the time of her murder, she was the lady behind the counter at night at the Casey's on Highway 3 at the edge of town.

She is very much unlike the women Mr Stevie seems to befriend through his job with the police. Women who work at dance clubs and bars. The ladies about town selling themselves for money and his personal blonde bimbo informants – cannot forget those. Julie would often complain to friends that he was always with one or the other of these women and defended them to her to the point of rage and violence. It is rumoured, for a quick blowjob and piece of ass in the back seat of his police car, Mr Stevie allows, not only this corrupt behaviour, but protects these women. Women who are selling drugs at their night dance jobs and prostituting while their children are at school.

She is ashamed and furious about this behaviour. So much so, she will no longer go around her family including her elderly parents. She cannot stand the pitying looks they give her or the questions they ask her about what they have heard he is up to. She tells him over and over she wants a divorce. She wants out of this charade of a marriage, but each time he refuses and beats her until she is unconscious. He keeps her drugged and locked up in her bedroom for days, making up stories that she is mentally ill. He will not allow even her parents to see her. And, thanks to his friends at the local police and sheriff's department as well as the local judge, there is nothing they can do about it!

She has tried to get away so many times and as a result, she has had countless threats and beatings imposed on her over the years. The events leading up to her death show exactly how desperate she was to get away. She moved into an apartment building in the dead of night while he was out of town. Out of town at what he called a conference, but what she knew was really a drug run; a trip to pick up the drugs that he sold out of the trunk of his police car. Supporting his retirement as he called it.

She chose a place with multiple apartments, a front door security system, and in a nearby city thinking she would be safer out of town and around a large community of people. Many times, she told her family and friends he always threatened to kill her if she left. This was part of her fear because she believed him. He did not hesitate to hit her, nor had he shown remorse with any of the violent behaviour he displayed towards her. She lived in her apartment one week before he got back to town from his alleged conference. Julie was found dead the same day he returned to find her not at home! There has never been a murder conviction for this crime. A large community broom has long since swept this under the rug!

Chapter 9

Mum/Mom's on Dope

This is happening so much more than anyone is aware of, parents trading their children for their next high. Recently it was reported that Indiana ranks second only to Kentucky for cases of child abuse; what a wake-up call and very fitting for this book.

When I first met Sue, she was in the office for a backache and was barely 18 years old. She was a high school dropout, non-social and had multi-coloured unkept hair. Sue had a history of bipolar disorder, diagnosed several years ago by an unknown source. Now I wonder if the provider that diagnosed Sue's bipolar disorder knew what was happening to her at home. She was in and out of the office for several years with the normal ailments for someone her age and often accompanied by mom and dad as she doesn't drive. Mom and dad are patients of the office as well so catching a ride with them was easy.

Mom and dad talk about Sue not getting out, being very moody, having now gotten involved with questionable people. Getting pregnant while not wed and giving birth to a child. Sue is in her early 20s now and a seemingly good mother herself. Mom and dad continue to worry about her not working, trying to raise a child on her own, being anti-social, and having boyfriend problems. They admit she has limited supports, both family and social. They are urging her to come in and talk to me to see what's troubling her so much.

Recently at an office visit, Sue came alone for the first time and wanted to discuss her mental health. She starts by telling me she's not sleeping much. She says she is stressed over her finances and trying to make ends meet, and says she is having difficulty holding or finding a job because she is so nervous and paranoid around people. Sue says she feels like everyone knows all about her less-than-perfect homelife and her past. She says she has episodes of weeping and separates herself from everyone. I can't come out of my bedroom, I can't go shopping, I can't even take a walk. I will take the baby out to the porch as long as we do not have traffic on the street; she says.

Sue says she cannot talk to her mother as her mother is part of the problem and refuses to believe her actions haven't caused any distress among her children. "Mother was taking so much different dope and eating bath salts, she cannot remember anything that she said or did to us. I cannot approach the subject because she gets mad. And Dad will not get involved or allow us to say anything to her; he is afraid of her!"

Sue asks then that I never tell her mother who is on her chart as her emergency contact, what we discuss, and I agree. Sue says; I don't want to hurt her feelings because now she is clean and trying. Sue goes on to tell me she experiences episodes of fear and panic related to her past and problems she endured at a much younger age. I encourage her to talk and express her concerns so I can better understand what has happened to her and get her the appropriate type of treatment.

She says her parents were partially separated when she was 11 or 12 years of age. Sue and her siblings lived with the father because her mother was having so many problems and strung out on all kinds of dope. Sue says her mother was not stable and on drugs including bath salts that made her crazy. She says; my mom would take me and my older sister with her when my dad wasn't around and make my older sister go into hotel rooms with all kinds of different men she didn't know. My mom made her have sex and she would get paid for it in money and drugs.

One after another would come to the car window and hand my mom money and go into the hotel room where my older sister was while we waited in the car at the door of the hotel room. Mom would park close enough to hear screams and watch the door. This happened almost every weekend for the three years my mom was on dope. Chris, my sister, was only 15. My mom didn't seem to care if she came out crying or with a black eye or bruised all to pieces. She just laughed it off and told her to rest for the next one, saying some men like it rough!

She would make my sister dress up in fancy dresses or nighties. She made her wear high heels and tons of makeup. My mother didn't even seem to care when my sister was left in a puddle of blood on the bed because a man she didn't know roughed her up, raped her and tried to put a walking cane inside her butt! Once again mom laughed it off and told Chris to clean herself up and made her keep going until the last of the men had gone.

Consequently, Chris now has five children who all have a different father and she is only 33 years old. Sue says she feared every time her mother would pull up outside their father's home. She would pretend to be ill or hide from her mother. Sue says she was afraid to go with her mother because she didn't know what her mother wanted. She didn't know what would happen to her or where she would end up. Sue says she always feared her mother would make her go into the hotel with her sister or with some man she didn't know. Still today Sue fears strangers – both men and women. She panics when she goes out into a crowd. Sue says she has a hard time believing her mother can't remember anything she did. She says they argue a lot because Sue thinks she doesn't want to admit what she did. If they don't talk about it, it didn't happen.

Sue says her mother would beat her father with either her fists in the face or anything else that she could get her hands on when he tried to stop her from taking either her or her sister. Sue tells me she witnessed her mother beat her father so badly, she did not recognise him. Sue says she has witnessed her mother hit her father with a wooden stick, metal bar from the back of the car, and even throw glass bottles at him. Sue says she never wanted to take on her older brothers and in fact, ran over my oldest brother Dan because he tried to stop the car. She took just us girls because she knew we were afraid of her and would do whatever she told us to just to avoid getting beaten by her or left at the side of the road in the middle of the night miles or towns from home!

Sue goes on to say that her mother would steal anything in the house while they were gone including food from the refrigerator, their clothes or anything else she could sell. Sue says her father would try to take care of them, but he could hardly feed them as her mother would take their food stamps and sell them for drugs. Her mother would steal her father's checks and not come home for weeks at a time, leaving them with very little to eat and they went several months without electricity and water.

"Mom would not feed the dog and wouldn't let us feed the dog; it was so starved, it died," Sue says and starts to weep. "We hid and buried it late at night so no-one could see." She tells me it was so bad that they only had left-over spaghetti in the refrigerator with green mould on it and she had to eat it because there was nothing else in the house to eat.

I missed a lot of school those years and couldn't tell anyone because I was afraid of my mom. I made myself throw up every day to avoid her and stay home from school so nobody would talk to me.

I wasn't allowed to have friends and now I don't want them; she says. I don't know why they wonder what is wrong with me, it's everything I went through. I felt so alone; she says. There was no-one to help me. My mom was drugged up someplace all the time, and Dad didn't have any money for food or anything else.

Sue says she believes everyone knows what she had to do to survive and this causes her shame. She has problems with social situations, feeling like everyone is looking at her. She has had to quit several jobs because when she gets to work in a social environment, she gets nauseated and cannot stop vomiting. Sue tells me she vomited every day for a month when she started her last fast-food position and was fired after only 30 days.

She says her mother would constantly threaten her father with the welfare and taking the kids if he told anybody what she was doing. Sue says her father was afraid not only for himself, but he feared the loss of his children and what else might happen to them. Sue says her mother got to the point of living in her car and not only selling her sister for money but prostituting herself to get high.

Sue says this did not end until her father took her and her siblings and left the state for several months. They went to live with family so they could eat and have a roof over their head without worrying if her mom was going to come in fighting, high or try to hurt them. She says her father was her only stability and she watched her beat him so many times until his face was bloody. He finally took them away so she couldn't find them.

She says she was offered help and did see a child psychologist for several years but never really could stop feeling as if everyone knows what happened to her and that she was forced to eat mouldy food. Sue says her family can't talk about it at home because it gets everyone upset, and her mother can't remember so they act like it never happened.

Sue goes on to say, but I can't forget it. I feel like I'm haunted and when I go out, people are pointing and laughing at me. They wonder why I stay in my room with the baby, it's because I am afraid and ashamed, and they don't get it.

I suggest psychiatry and psychological counsel for Sue and urge her to attend as well as medications to dampen the anxiety she is stricken with. Her family does see a difference when Sue is compliant with treatment but unfortunately, she fails to maintain her own health and wellness. With non-compliance, Sue forces herself to relive her stress daily and remain a victim of child abuse as the result of her mother's use of drugs. Remaining hidden in her room, clinging to her young child as if it were a lifeline, unemployed and uneducated, Sue cannot see past today.

Chapter 10

My Husband Had a Vasectomy and I Am Pregnant

Tammy, age 45 at the time, comes into the office with the complaint of missed periods. She says she is late with her period by about 8 weeks. Tammy goes on to say she did a home pregnancy test and it was positive.

I can't tell my husband Tom because he had a vasectomy after June our daughter was born, so the baby is not his!

June, who is now 12 or 13 years old, is with her mother today and very aware her mother may be pregnant. Aware this pregnancy is not a child of her father, but she says very little, she just allows Tammy to direct her conversation and speak for her. I am almost positive this is not the only secret Tammy shares with her young daughter who just seems to agree with everything her mother says, regardless if it is right or wrong.

We move forward with a serum pregnancy test and it is in fact positive. Tammy is new to the practice and a transplant from another city coming back home to be with her parents. She goes on to say they came back home to New Castle because Tom lost his job. Tammy subsequently travels and has in the office with her today a Latino man, who I am sure is not her husband. She doesn't introduce him, just says he is a close family friend – the father of the baby perhaps!

Tammy asks for the plan B pill to abort her pregnancy and as she is new to me and greater than 8 weeks pregnant, I refuse and send her to Planned Parenthood in Anderson, IN for further evaluation and treatment. Once evaluated by Planned Parenthood, Tammy is found to be 12 weeks pregnant and gets an abortion one third of the way through her pregnancy. A pregnancy that did not involve her husband, and she has also swore her 12-year-old daughter, who is supposed to be the daughter of Tom, to secrecy regarding the baby and the abortion. She says she is experiencing a great deal of bleeding and it is 14 days post abortion, and I suggest she contact Planned Parenthood again as they are the ones who ended her pregnancy.

Upon return to the clinic for follow-up on her abortion, Tammy is found to have been carrying two foetus and one of them remains in the uterus and must be removed with a second procedure. Tammy continues to proceed with the procedure and rid herself of the second of the two babies she was carrying. She tells me June, her daughter, was with her and was able to watch the procedure, and now she cannot sleep and awakens crying in the night, dreaming over and over someone is trying to kill her. Tammy says they found her in the middle of the kitchen floor with a small paring knife cutting holes in her skin and running her hand through the blood.

I am worried about her; Tammy says, but not worried enough to allow her to see psychiatry, counselling or tell her father what she has witnessed. Instead, Tammy suggests medications for this 12-year-old who has apparently been traumatised by her mother's actions. I refuse to medicate this child and continue to ask questions regarding other things that may have contributed to June and her nightmares. She says; well, Tom and I are fighting right now, and we must move from our home because we cannot keep up on the payment. June will have to change schools once again and this seems to upset her; she will have changed schools three times this year and it's only April.

Again, Tammy refuses to believe she has taken part in causing her daughter such trauma and once more suggests she be put on Adderall of all things. Tammy and June are sent to counselling and behaviour health. After several months, Tammy returns to the office without June, who has apparently taken her own life. Tammy is sobbing now, telling me how she found June in the middle of the bathroom floor trying to give herself an abortion with a kitchen knife.

Tammy says she was screaming at me; I didn't tell, I didn't tell! And then just crumpled into a pile. Tammy tells me June bled to death before she could be properly treated. Tammy goes on to say; I cleaned her up and put her back to bed for the evening, I didn't know how bad it was or what she had done to herself. I gave her a sedative to calm her down, hoping she would sleep through the night; I thought it would be okay if she got some rest.

Tom had started driving a truck and was gone for days at a time. I thought no-one would have to know because it is only me and her there at night. Tammy goes on sobbing and says, I drove her crazy. I read her diary while I thought she was sleeping. She described my abortion, my bleeding, and says I didn't care about the baby, I just wanted it dead, so I did not have to be bothered with it. June entered in her diary every day since the abortion how she felt lucky to be wanted because if she wasn't, I would have killed her too.

June described what she had seen during the abortion as a bloody baby doll sucking its thumb. Not big enough to hurt anyone she entered, just a tiny baby that wasn't wanted by anyone. I can't tell Daddy, she wrote over and over, he will hate Mommy more than he already does.

Chapter 11
Left

B. Ruth comes to the practice from Georgia as her last residence. She is a middle-aged pleasant lady with blonde hair and glasses. B. Ruth has grown children of her own and several small grandchildren. As we move forward into her history, she tells me she was left at a roadside truck stop in 1975 by her mother; she was 7 years old.

B. Ruth says; I remember she (mom) was dressed up to go someplace and told me to pack some clothes, we wouldn't be back for a day or two and to get my favourite toy to take along. I was happy because she never took me with her when she left, and she never let me take my toys out of the house. I remember this must be something special or a surprise just for me.

We had been in the car for a while, it seemed like all day to me, and then we finally stopped along the highway to use the restroom and stretch our legs as she put it. I went into the bathroom by myself, I was a big girl of 7 and could find my way in and out of the bathroom alone. And I did not want to disappoint my mother as this was the first time she let me come along.

When I came back to the car, which was a wood-panelled station wagon with brown interior and a terrible radio that played more hissing noise and static than music, she was gone, and my things were left sitting where the car had been. I froze in fear. I had never been left alone especially along the highway with strangers. My mother had abandoned me at the rest stop in the late afternoon, about the time you notice it will soon be dark. I panic and start running around the entire rest stop asking strangers, Did you see my mother, did you see where she went, will she be back for me? Finally, exhausted, cold and scared, I sat on my pile of things in the rest stop parking lot and began to cry.

I must have fallen asleep in a heap on my pile because I was shaken awake by an older man with grey hair, long grey beard, no teeth and a bright orange jacket like one you see highway workers wear. He was telling me, Wake up, what are you doing here, and asking if I ran away from home. I awoke frightened in the dark in a strange place. I was cold and hungry and scared to death; this man made my fear escalate to the point of being terrified and panicked. I remember he looked around the empty lot and grabbed me by the arm – I was frozen with fear. I tried to scream but nothing came out. I was kicking to get away from this stranger who was dragging me by one outstretched arm. He was pulling me through the wet grass over the hill behind the rest stop.

When we got to the bottom of the hill, it was very dark, the glow of the rest stop lights seemed so far away, and I couldn't hear anything but the hum of a car on the highway now and then. He stood me up square in front of him with his hands on my shoulders, my dress ripped half off my body, my shoes now gone somewhere in the grass. He started talking to me in a hushed mean voice saying, 'Run away from home, ae? Were they mean to you, did you have a sneaky uncle?' By now he is grinning, and his no teeth were showing. He was grabbing hard on my shoulders with both hands stretched out between us and then with a jerk, he pushed me down flat on my back. My dress came up over my face and before I knew what happened, he was on top of me, holding my dress over my face with his arms. I started to scream and cry. I tried to wiggle away from him, but he was holding me down with my face covered in my dress and grabbing at my underwear, pulling it off me. I kept kicking and screaming; he wouldn't stop.

He kept whispering to me like I knew what he was talking about. He kept saying, That's a girl, keep kicking, I like a woman with spunk. I was not a woman; I was a 7-year-old child who was being raped by a total stranger in an open field in the middle of the night. I was alone, scared and now scarred for the rest of my life. This was not the surprise I expected when my mother told me I could come along this time! He kept grabbing at me everywhere. I was jerking and trying to kick, but it was useless, he was way too big and heavy for me to get away.

"He jerked my dress even higher and started to bite my breasts; all I could do was scream and cry. I tried to bite his arm, but he pushed it further in my face and my nose started bleeding. My teeth were pushed into my lip, hurting me that much more. He was now clutching and grabbing between my legs, my private parts that I learned at school no one is supposed to touch. He was saying things to me like, 'You want it, don't you, little girl? I will teach you, little girl, little runaway wants to be a big girl on her own.'

He started to rub his body against me, and I started screaming as loud as I could, Stop! I didn't run away, my mommy left me here, stop, stop, and then he was lying on top of me, his fingers in my private and he was poking at me hurting me. Well, what do you know, she's a fresh baby; he said; lucky me. he kept on whispering; I'll make it a night to remember as long as you live.

I don't know what happened next; I woke up and the sun was up. I was back on my pile of things at the rest stop and a policeman was shaking me. 'Wake up, honey, what are you doing here?' he was saying. The lady who cleans the bathrooms apparently found me at 5am in the parking lot when she came to work and called the police.

I remember I could hardly move; I was so sore. My dress was ripped half off my body. I had no shoes, no socks, dried blood all over me. I started vomiting the minute I stood up. I could hardly stand and walk as they ushered me toward the bathrooms inside the rest area shelter. I had cuts and bruises all over me. My butt had scrapes and bruises all over it. The woman gasped when she started to help me clean up because she could see the handprints in black and blue all over my body. I remember she started to tear up and pulled me close to her and held me while we both cried. This was 1975 and she helped me change my dress, get cleaned up, and the policeman took me to my grandparents' house; that became my new home.

I didn't really see my mother too much after that as my grandmother would not allow her to come and visit. I spent ages 7-14 getting molested by my grandfather before he died. I was not able to tell my grandmother because he said it would kill her. I was a child and did not want my grandmother, who saved me from horror, to die. I am over 50 years old now, a grown woman with children of my own, and I continue to be haunted by a stranger in the night. I endure lasting pain and emotional trauma daily, and I need a light on to sleep. I fear traveling alone still today and rarely go out of town by myself if at all.

Chapter 12

My Brother, My Nephew

Mora is a quiet lady, unsuspecting of any history out of the normal. She shares her story to heal and relieve future generations of her family of the burden of keeping such vile secrets as they have in the past.

Mora tells me the story of her family and her sisters, and their will to survive. She says it started when she was 5 or 6 years old and her mother ran away, leaving her and her five sisters and three brothers with their father. Her father was an alcoholic who could hardly hold any type of steady job and her mother was a nurse. Her father repeatedly would come in drunk and as with so many alcoholic cases, beat on her mother until she could no longer stand it and left. She left the 8 young children with the father and moved to another state to get away. He would never grant her a divorce and in the sixties, it was not that uncommon.

Mora tells me her five sisters ranged from ages 4 to 12 years of age at that time, approximately 1965-1970. She tells me they rarely went to school. She says they had very little in the way of outside contact as the father would not allow them to leave the house. He would not allow them to have friends or associate with other family members outside their immediate home.

She says she was placed on a strict curfew and made to get up at 6am and to bed at 6pm, regardless of the day or time of the year. She says her father would come in every night drunk and wanted to fight at first with the boys. She says he would pull them out of their rooms and beat them as if they were men. He would accuse them of knowing where their mother was and keeping it a secret from him. He would try to make them feel responsible for their mother running away, abandoning them.

After several months of beating the boys on a regular basis, he changed and started to focus his attention on the girls. He would come in late at night drunk and pull one of the girls out of the bedroom to sleep with him in his room. All the girls shared a bedroom and a bed, each very aware of the other coming and going in the night. Eventually, it got to the point he was molesting each of the girls on a regular basis. Mora says he was coming to the bedroom late at night not only when he was drunk but every night after the house had settled down and everyone was supposed to be sleeping.

He would choose a different sibling every night to be his companion in his big bed as he used to say. The girls would pretend to be sleeping when they heard him make the climb up the creaking stairway leading to their room, because they knew what was going to happen. He was sick and they all agreed, but they experienced such fear and shame, it paralysed them from telling anyone. Mora's older sister was normally the one he chose as she was very attractive and the most developed of the sibling girls. Mora was the next to the youngest of the siblings and was one of the last to be able to leave the house as an adult and get away from her father and the molestation she endured for many years.

The girls did eventually, after much time had gone by, tell their mother what was happening, but it was too late to prevent any abuse. They were now all grown women and out of the house. Velvet was the youngest of the girls and the last to leave; she became pregnant at 12 and lost this child to unknown causes. She again became pregnant at 14 and gave birth to her father's child. This child was both Mora's brother and nephew. This was a heart-wrenching event that became one of the family's secrets for years to come.

Soon after the birth of this child, several of the siblings were able to confront the father and speak to local school authorities as they were all taken from class and brought together by a counsellor who questioned the pregnancy of this 14-year-old child. The father was charged with child molestation and placed in prison for a time. According to Mora, not long enough to make any difference or ease the pain he had caused his children.

Mora says she developed a very strong bond with the child of her younger sister and they in fact grew close enough to confide in each other. Over the years as Josh grew up to be a teenager and young adult, he was known to have anxiety and depression issues that caused him much pain. He was withdrawn from almost everyone but a cousin of his same age and Mora.

Mora says Josh was at an age he wanted to know who his father was because he lived his life without one, and Velvet says she did not know who his father was. Velvet repeatedly told Josh he was the result of a fling at a party. Unsure if Josh knew of the sexual abuse and incest that took place in the family, Mora started asking Josh questions about his mother and father. He had heard from other family members that his grandfather had molested his mother and she had gotten pregnant without ever having any boyfriend to speak of.

Mora went on to say Josh confronted his grandfather once the old man was out of jail and asked him to take a paternity test and he refused. This happened over and over. It ended with the old man telling Josh to mind his own business, go away and never come back to his house. All the while Velvet telling Josh, "He is not your dad, he is your grandfather and that would be sick." Knowing in fact that Josh was her father's son.

Velvet herself has been in and out of various mental institutions trying to deal with the trauma of her childhood but was never successful. Josh was distraught most of the time about the possibility of his grandfather being his father. This situation was made worse as other family members would tease him and call him hillbilly brother and daddy's son, heaping more shame upon this 21-year-old than he could handle.

Mora says she did tell Josh he belonged to her father in a phone conversation they had right before Josh killed himself. She says; I could not stand it any longer, watching everyone drive this kid crazy, make fun of him and mock him. The whole thing was getting to be too much to bear for me, his aunt and sister. I cannot imagine what was going on in his mind.

Josh was found the next day having shot himself in the head. He left no note.

Chapter 13

We Robbed Wendy's and Got Away with It!

It was an inside job to say the least; Buffy exclaims almost laughing. She is so excited telling me her story and about her success. She is very proud that she outsmarted the local New Castle, Indiana Police Department and arrogant dim-witted detectives. Buffy says; It has been several years since I worked for and robbed Wendy's fast-food chain. No one is the wiser that it was me who did it! she says. Her face is flushed pink and her grin is from ear to ear as she tells me the story. She is obviously proud of her accomplishment and ill-gotten gains because she is bubbly, smiling and even relaxed telling me of the events of the robbery.

Buffy is a middle-aged woman; she is fifty or sixtyish. She is not the young teenager or grandmother type you would expect to work at a fast-food restaurant or to be so deviant in nature. She appears a little on the rough side at first glance. She has an array of tattoos covering her exposed limbs with slightly dishevelled clothes and hair most of the time. She speaks in a quiet demeanour and at times seems almost cunning and innocent. She tells you just enough and knows when to shut up or shut down her conversation if she goes too far or says too much.

Her closest friends are afraid of her, telling me, "She is very vengeful and doesn't care who she hurts, so please never tell her I talk about her," they say. She has been in and out of jail and prison herself throughout her life but rarely speaks of this. Her long-time closest friends do know about the robbery. Buffy is called a slinger by people who know her the best! When I asked what this means, I was told she helps people sell drugs as the middleman for a profit. Transporting them from one place to another and/or one person to another and so on; the buyer and seller may never really know one another.

Buffy has dirty blonde hair with some grey peeking through. She wears her hair in a variety of long and short cuts and colours. Today she has a pageboy cut and some added pink colour at the bangs. She tells me a friend's daughter who happens to be in beauty school did it for her free of charge for the experience. Buffy is much heavier than she should be but is attempting to diet and having some success at it. She dresses casual on a continuous basis, pants only. She is outgoing and friendly to converse with, not the type you would expect to have this obvious dark side.

She has young adult children that she is setting the example for. An example that includes murder, robbery and drugs. This shows as her children are both in and out of trouble with the law. In fact, her son is currently in prison for murder. A second murder that he has been involved with in the past two or three years. This time she swears he was just the driver only and knew nothing of the robbery and killing that were pre-planned. Her friends tell an entirely different story, saying she knew everything that was happening before it ever took place. Easily willing to kill for less than 1,000 dollars; this is an outward indication that these people have no respect for life. It's apparent by in and out of jail histories that the mobster mentality has not proven a family friend to them. Buffy's friends tell me she tries to direct and correct the actions of her son that are deviant, telling him he should have done it this way, not that way. Never telling him he should not have done it, period. Only saying he should not have gotten caught!

Buffy continues to tell me she was working at Wendy's fast-food chain several years ago and had been there for several months without incident. She says she befriended the store manager, consequently the gal who hired her after being recommended by long-time family and friends. Buffy says this girl was a very young woman, overweight and insecure, who had few friends outside of work. She goes on to say; It was obvious she could be easily manipulated by the way workers altered their schedules and got away with it.

After several months of working with her, having lunch together and meeting up after work for events, I asked her to allow me to work the night shift. She happily made me night shift leader and closer of the store. I was my own boss; Buffy says. I did pretty much whatever I wanted to and had her blessing. I had won over her trust and I knew it. If someone complained about me, she was quick to defend me at every turn, so I thought I had it made. Come to find out, I did. I worked there almost another year after the robbery.

The store was taking in several thousand dollars every night and Saturdays turned out the be the best day of the week for cash. Each Saturday, I would evaluate the cash and keep track of which Saturday of the month we took in the most money. I also kept track of which day of the week and month we had the most cash on hand in the store at the end of the day. My evaluation proved the weekends at the first of the month were the largest money-makers, she said.

One evening, I was joking at a party with some friends and spontaneously said, 'I think I'm going to heist the store!' People looked up at me puzzled and gasped at first. A long-time friend of mine, and someone who also new Tessa the store manager, spoke up and said, 'I'm in,' and we all laughed it off after that remark. Later that night when I got home, I knew I was going to do it; I was going to rob the store. Now I had my accomplice, my boyfriend's cousin Bruce. Making several thousand dollars in just a few minutes seemed like a no-brainer to me. They owed it to me, coming in early, staying late, putting up with lazy teenagers. I knew Tessa the manager would never suspect me as the robber either. Neither would she suspect Bruce, her uncle-in-law and my accomplice.

I started planning in my head which Saturday I would fake getting robbed. It would be an unknown individual who robbed the store I would say to the police when questioned. But this unknown individual would really be my accomplice, Bruce. I decided to go with the first Saturday of the month in December; this was just a few weeks away. I knew that we would have a lot of cash in the building since we did the year before. The security cameras had malfunctioned around Thanksgiving and were not working. I knew they wouldn't be back up for weeks. Christmas was a crazy time at the restaurant because of the holidays. We get traffic from people out doing their Christmas shopping wanting to eating out. People getting their monthly checks who always increased revenue on the first weekend of the month. And of course, it was Saturday, the busiest day of the week.

Late at night when everything settles down around town, she said was a perfect time to get robbed. My boyfriend and his daughter would be having a meal at the restaurant that evening. And there is always a couple who meet after their 3-11 shift for coffee; I would be able to count on them as witnesses to the robbery as well. The young kids who worked with me would also be witness to the robbery and since I am being robbed, they would never expect it was me who was robbing the place.

I always start counting and changing out the cash drawers around midnight at the end of my shift. So, this night I did just that without any disruption to routine. We had taken in almost 30,000 dollars the day of the robbery. I was so excited, I only had to give Bruce 2,000 and a half gallon of vodka for helping me.

The drawers were counted, and the money was placed in the bags for bank deposit as usual. I put the bags in the safe, gave it a twist and locked the door behind me. I made my way back out to the counter as routine as the night before and had the kid working the grill start on a chicken sandwich, that I would take home. I always took home a chicken sandwich; free food, a benefit of working in the restaurant, I felt.

It was 12:15 am after a busy Saturday night and time to get robbed! Bruce came in, dressed in all black. He had a black hood covering his head and plain black shoes on his feet that consequently had a 3" heel, disguising his height. You could see nothing of him from head to toe, only black. His eyes were shaded with mirrored sunglasses.

He pulled a gun from the pocket of his overcoat. An overcoat that was three sizes too big and all a part of the plan. I figured using this overcoat you would not be able to tell he was really a very thin man. The car he had gotten out of was in the drive-through, seemingly another normal transaction taking place.

He pointed the gun at me and handed me a note. The note was written sloppily with black marker on bright yellow paper. The note said, It's a robbery, do as I say, and nobody gets hurt! He fired one shot into the floor. The gunshot was a blank, but it was just as loud as the real thing and did the job quite well without leaving any residual findings for the police. As planned, the gunshot had gotten the attention of everybody in the place. They all came running to the front counter towards me and this man wearing all black holding a gun in my face.

The teenage girl working at the drive-through window and the two boys from the back of the store were now crowded together a few feet away from me still behind the counter. The couple having coffee and my boyfriend with his daughter had gathered in the corner at the front of the store on the other side of the counter. I was waving the note in the air with my hands above my head, just as frantically as I possibly could to make the whole thing seem as real as possible.

I started yelling, we're getting robbed! and then I quickly proceeded to motion the group of patrons to come behind the counter, gathered them with the employees, then herded them down the hall to the back freezer. The robber following closely behind me, pointing the gun in my back for show. When they were all in the freezer, I closed and locked the door, locking them in. Once they were secure and could not see me, I started screaming and crying out; no, don't hit me, please! as we made our way back towards the front office, Bruce continuing to point and shove the gun in my back, in case someone was looking out the freezer window at us. With the events unfolding so quickly, they had not noticed it was me who had ordered them to walk to the back of the building and get in the freezer.

Once inside the office, Bruce dropped the gun to his side. I opened the safe and placed the bagged money into a briefcase that I had brought to work several days before in a large shopping bag as part of gift exchange night. I locked and handed the loaded briefcase to Bruce. Then I gave him a quick shove to get him moving. Stepping in front of him, he again points the gun at my back, and I lead him down the hall, past the freezer, to the back door. He fired one last shot as he exited the building. He got into the car that was still waiting in the drive-through just a few steps from the back door. Just like that, he was gone without a trace.

I went back inside and opened the freezer door, allowing everyone inside to exit. Obviously shaken and still in shock regarding the incident, not much was said. Once we checked everyone to be sure we were all okay, I called the police.

I asked everyone to stay but my boyfriend gave me a quick squeeze, asked if I was okay, and said I am getting my daughter out of here and left with her in tow. She was screaming and crying by now as they left the building. The older couple asked if I was okay and sat back down to wait for the police. The obviously stunned teens locked the doors and sat to wait with the couple and I for the police to arrive.

Once seated and feeling calmer, I called the store manager. I told her we had been robbed and that the police were on the way. She asked were we all okay and said to close the store for the rest of the night. She said she would be there as soon as possible. It is now approximately 1am. When the police arrived, we unlocked the doors to allow them in as everyone remains shaken and leery.

Buffy says; by now I am crying and clinging to anyone, seeming as distraught as everybody else in the room. The police asked questions about the robber, what he looked like, what build he had, how tall was he. The response was a hefty man in an overcoat, sunglasses, and cowboy boots. He was described as approximately six feet tall, three inches taller than he was without women's boots on. Boots that he will never wear again. She laughs telling me this. She goes on to say it took forever to get Bruce to agree to wear those boots. We joke about his high heels still today.

He was described as an angry man with a deep voice, yelling and screaming orders to us all to move and get in the freezer. The reality is, he never said anything. He just handed me the note as planned. He was described as threatening to shoot us all if we didn't do as he said. The parents of the teenagers have now entered the building along with Tessa the manager. Each questioned by the police. They asked Tessa what was taken. She reported the cash as the only thing missing.

I had to show them the places he shot the gun. The police looked for bullet holes, shell casings and anything else they could find but found nothing. He wore black gloves and I was careful to see that he didn't touch anything so they couldn't find any fingerprints. I had to walk them to the office and show them the safe that he never touched; again, they could not find any fingerprints.

When the police asked me for the note, I told them he grabbed it from my hand as he went out the back door. Everyone who was there then spoke up with something to say about it being yellow paper! I had shoved the note in my bra before letting everyone out of the freezer. It was in my handwriting and who knows whose fingerprints could have been on it; it was just a piece of construction paper I found lying around the house.

Tessa gave us all the next few days off to recover from the experience. When the police asked about the security cameras, she told them they were out of order. That they had been non-functioning since a power outage over Thanksgiving weekend and that they were supposed to be fixed next week.

There was no mention of my boyfriend and his daughter leaving shortly after the incident and they were never questioned by the police. The police detectives were in and out a few times after, but nothing was every solidified. They had no idea who robbed the store and still don't. Nobody knows it was me and Bruce except a few close family and friends. People I trust and people who trust me; she says. People who hate the police enough to never say a word; she says.

After I got home that night, Bruce was waiting with the briefcase full of cash sitting on my living room table. He hadn't even bothered to try and open the briefcase. I was the only one who had the key and knew exactly how much was inside. He was happy to get his $2,000 cut and half gallon of vodka that I stopped and got on the way home.

That night, I hid the money in the toes of my old shoes and in old pocketbooks that were never out of my closet. I hid part of it under the carpet in my bedroom; a corner piece that was loose where my nightstand sat. The place where I hid my credit cards from my kids.

Once back to work, there were a few days of unrest and concern from the teens who had been there that night. Talking about it and adding to the robbery with each story and person they told. Tessa was quick to console and call to check on us more often. She even got the security cameras fixed the next day after reporting the robbery to the owners. After several months, the robbery was forgotten by all it seemed. I quit that job at Wendy's to go to a better paying job at a local gas station. This was in July, seven months after the robbery.

I masterfully planned and got away with robbery! she said.

Chapter 14
Choked to Death

"My father choked my mother to death and hanged her over the clothesline in the basement when I was five years old," Cece says. "He never went to jail or got into any trouble for it because this is Henry County, Indiana, and they didn't do anything about domestic violence back then," she says. "I found her hanging by her neck on our basement clothesline," Cece says to me. This happened in 1962 in Henry County, Indiana. Women were treated just like the coloured folks or worse; they had no say in how things went. Women were deemed the property of their husband.

The New Castle State Hospital was in full swing with epileptic patients in 1962. Cece's family called these epileptics who were confined to the grounds of the state hospital 'helmet heads'. There was no real understanding of epilepsy at the time, so epileptics were treated as mentally ill individuals. People who were perfectly normal except for the occasional seizure were housed in mental institutions with the mentally insane and mentally handicapped at the New Castle State Hospital. They roamed the grounds freely. Each patient responsible for chores including taking care of the garden, doing laundry, working in the kitchens and so on.

Cece describes going for Sunday drives with her family and always going through the grounds of the state hospital. She lived only a few miles away with her mother, brother and father. "It was part of our Sunday outing," she says, "we would drive around the well-kept grounds and throw cigarettes out to the helmet heads. Dad was always drinking when he drove us around on Sunday; he kept his nipping whisky between his legs as he drove. He made a big deal to stop and throw out cigarettes each time we would come upon a group of hospital patients as we drove through. He would laugh and say, 'Look at the helmet heads all out for a walk today.'

"He always drank; not just on our Sunday drives but every day of the week. He called it his rheumatism medication when my mother would complain that he drank too much. 'I need this,' he would say. He would tell her, 'It helps my rheumatism and you don't want to see me in pain, do you?' Then he would let out an enormous drunken chuckle. She knew when to stop because when he got mad, he really got mad and could not seem to control himself. He was violent when he drank," she says. "But he refused to acknowledge what he had done when he was sober consequently, which was only until about one or two o'clock in the afternoon. I guess she was used to it," Cece says about her mother.

"We had just arrived back home after our usual Sunday drive. Dad would always say it was our church service and goodwill offering to throw cigarettes to the helmet heads on Sunday. He would not allow my mother to take us to church on Sunday or any other day of the week. He said preachers were just snake handlers peddling for money.

"That day when we got back home, he didn't go in the house, he just sat in the car and kept drinking. Mom said he had another bottle under the seat he wanted to finish off before he came in the house. 'He thinks he's doing something,' she said. 'The fool doesn't know I watched him hide the extra bottle of whisky under the seat before we left this morning.'

"Mother went about her business tidying up the house and fed us lunch. Sunday lunch always consisted of fried bologna sandwiches, a handful of potato chips and a little bottle of Coke. Sunday was the only day we could have a coke; Dad said coke will rot your teeth. With this, Mom would always turn her head from him to us, wrinkle her nose and make a funny face because she loved Coke and had a little bottle several times a day. As always, we ate every morsel and slowly sipped our cokes; this was my favourite part of our Sunday ritual.

"After we ate, my brother, who was just a year older, and I went to play on the front porch. When my father finally got out of the car and staggered to the house, we were still enjoying the mid-afternoon sun on this warm July day. He didn't say much as he walked past us towards the door leading inside our house. Our house was a big old white house Momma's daddy had given her when she got married. It had an upstairs, downstairs, a basement and an outside cellar where Daddy kept his liquor. 'The drunken cellar,' Mamma called it and always laughed because Daddy thought she was saying drunken sailor.

"He stopped and looked at my mother who was sitting beside us sorting beans on her lap. She would pull a handful from the pockets of her apron and snap them into pieces. She put the pieces into a big bowl on the floor in front of her. She used to always sit beside us on the porch when we played, her wooden rocker creaking on the floorboards as she gently rocked back and forth. She stayed close enough to be part of our conversations.

"My mother was a lovely woman," Cece says. "She was very pretty with long blonde hair that came down to her waist when she pulled it from the bun she wore most of the time. She was a thin woman who ate like a bird. She always wore makeup and fixed her hair in a neat bun at the nape of her neck. She got up before everyone else in the house to get dressed for the day and to start breakfast; she used to say it was her me time.

"She had lots of pretty dresses my grandma Sally, her mother, made for her. Daddy worked in a factory and never seemed to buy her anything, but said he kept a roof over our head and food in our mouth. He seemed to forget the house we lived in came from Grandpa, Mamma's daddy. Almost every week Grandma Sally would bring Mamma a new dress wrapped in brown paper and tied with a piece of pink ribbon. Pink was Mamma's favourite colour and had been since she was a little girl. Grandma says her childhood bedroom looked like a pink explosion of flowers.

"Mamma never seemed to get mad and she never yelled at us like Daddy did. She was always telling us how much she loved us, giving us hugs and kisses on the cheek. She would play with us outside and read to us at night before bed. I never understood why Daddy would get so mad at her. In my eyes, Mamma was perfect.

After a few minutes of him standing there glaring at her, she looked up from her beans and asked did he need help getting in the house. He yelled something like, 'Hell no, I don't need help, woman.' He was always calling her woman and I never heard him say he loved her. She shoved the beans back into her apron pockets, stood up and moved the bowl from her feet to the table beside her rocker. She gave us a quick glance, grinned and winked to us then disappeared inside the house. Daddy followed close behind her.

The door shut and you could hear it lock. I don't know who locked it, him or her. But they were both in the house now and the door was locked. We couldn't get to her when she started yelling and screaming. I could hear something crash to the floor. When we peeked in the front door window, we could see the big green lamp that always sat beside the front door smashed all over the floor. Smashed right there in front of the door; pieces of green glass were everywhere.

"This time it was different, my brother and I both knew it. They never broke anything before when they quarrelled. He yelled when he looked our way and found our faces pressed against the front door glass. 'You kids get away from that window before I come out there and move you myself!' he shouted. We moved away from the glass but only to the side window behind Mamma's rocker so we could watch without being seen.

"My mother was standing at the wooden stairway; I couldn't tell if she was going upstairs or down to the basement. Her face was red, her eyes were swollen and wide open, and she was crying. She had blood coming from her left eye and her nose was bleeding. She had blood all over her mouth and chin. The right sleeve of her bright yellow dress that Grandma Sally had made last week was torn to her wrist and the buttons on the front were open to her belly. We could see her bra and her slip. We could also see the big red mark on her chest and the blood on her dress. We had never seen Mamma like this before – half naked, bloody and crying.

As we continued to peer through the window at them, we could see him hitting her, slamming her to the floor, kicking her in the head and face. He would knock her down and then pick her up to only hit her again until she was on the floor. My brother and I were both crying now, hitting the windows and yelling for him to stop. But he wouldn't, he didn't even look up at us, he just kept hitting her.

"We could hardly hear anything, he seemed to be yelling at her. Finally, when she could not stand alone any longer, he picked her up, propped her against the wall and put his hands around her neck. We watched him holding my mother to the wall with his hands around her neck until she just felt limp. Her head slumped to the side and then he let go. She seemed to slide down the wall into a pile on the floor.

"He didn't pick up her body like before, he just kicked her until she was at the edge of the steps leading to the basement. He didn't stop kicking her until her body disappeared down the steps.

"Then he turned toward us and started for the front door. My brother and I both started running off the porch and didn't stop running until we were well into the nearby woods where we knew he couldn't find us. We could see the front porch from the edge of the trees and bushes we were hiding under, but he couldn't see us; he just kept yelling at us to come here. Finally, he turned back to the house and sat in a chair on the front porch, waiting. He just sat there for what seemed like forever. We watched from under the bushes as he went back in the house for a while and then came back out to the porch without my mother. Again, he sat down and seemed to just fall asleep, or pass out as Mamma called it.

"We laid hid under the bushes until almost dark and then went back to the house. Dad was still sleeping on the porch when we went inside to find Mamma. The house was a wreck. The furniture was turned over and there was glass everywhere. I had never seen so much blood; the blood seemed to cover everything, even the walls. We looked everywhere for Mamma with no luck. Finally, my brother told me to check the basement and he would go to the back porch and look. As I started down the basement steps, I was in shock at the blood everywhere. I had to step here and there to avoid stepping in it.

"As I walked into the dark basement and flipped the light on, I could immediately see Mamma. She was hanging by her neck over the clothesline, right along with the towels she had hung up earlier. Her chin seemed to be stuck to her chest. She was just hanging there, still. I started to yell and cry, 'Mamma! Mamma!' but she didn't move. Her face was black and swollen with blood still smeared all over. Her dress was gone now, completely torn away from her body. She had nothing on but her slip, her shoes and her stockings that were still on her feet.

"I tried to touch her to get her to wake up, but she didn't move, she just seemed to swing back and forth. I was still screaming, 'Mamma, Mamma, wake up!' when my brother came into the room. We both tried to move her and help her down but couldn't; she seemed so heavy and stiff like she was attached to the clothesline. My brother told me to stay with her and he would call Grandma Sally and Grandpa to come over and help us.

"He called my grandparents. I don't know what he told them, but they were there in just a few minutes; they only lived a few miles down the road from us. When my brother brought my grandparents into the basement, my grandmother gasped and fell to the floor immediately upon seeing my mother hanging on the clothesline. My grandfather told him to go call the police; 'use the emergency numbers taped to the bottom of the phone,' he said. My mother kept the phone number to the police with the word 'help' taped to the bottom of our phone and told us to call if we ever needed help.

"My father didn't wake up until the sheriff's car pulled into the driveway with its lights and siren blaring. He followed my grandfather who had been waiting on the porch and the sheriff to the basement where my mother was still hanging. My grandmother had awoken and was standing by my mother, clutching her legs and wailing. The minute my father stepped into the room, my grandmother started yelling, 'You killed my daughter, you drunken fool!'

"My grandfather turned to look at my father; he had not realised my father had awakened from his drunken stupor and followed them to the basement. My grandfather raised his fist and began to yell at my father as well. Grandpa was now crying and moving forward towards my father. The sheriff stepped in between them and asked my grandfather what happened.

"My mother remained hanging in the basement while the sheriff asked questions. He spoke to all of us; myself, my brother, my grandparents and my dad. Finally, someone came in another big black car and took my mother's lifeless body away. My brother and I went home with my grandparents to live.

"My father never spoke to me again after that day. He never went to jail and never got punished for killing my mother in a drunken rage. My grandfather did make him move from our house. He did have a limited relationship with my brother at the end of his life. He was without question the worst type of alcoholic," she says.

Chapter 15

It Was a Hot Shot

Mr Smyth tells me today of his wife and her recent demise. He says the newspaper and the police think she committed suicide. But I know her brother really killed her with a "drug overdose". I am beside myself, he says. I thought she had stopped using drugs. She had been at the house for several days; we were trying to work out our problems. As you know we have been having marital problems for months, but we had started to get close again. I thought this was finally behind us. I thought she was coming back home to stay and be a family again.

He goes on to say; we had a great week. She came over and we hung out on the couch watching movies. I rubbed her feet and checked her toes because that's where she always shot herself up. Between the toes, so no one would see the marks; he said. She had no marks any place and I thought she was clean. I thought the drugs were going to be a thing of the past. After all, she had done nothing all week.

The day she was hit by the train, she had been at my house all morning. We ate breakfast, spent time with our grandchildren, and even discussed gaining custody of them because their mother had started down the wrong path and they were being neglected, we thought. Later that afternoon, her brother Ritchie and sister-in-law Deena text her to see if she wanted to come over to their place for a while. Sherly didn't drive and they said they would come and get her; she quickly said yes.

"I didn't know it was the last time I would see her alive or we would not have argued. I told her not to go, she didn't listen. 'It's harmless,' she said. 'We're just going to hang out, no big deal.' She was ready to go when they pulled up out front to pick her up. I know her brother Ritchie makes his own meth in his house; you can smell it when you walk in the yard. He only gets away with it because he does roof jobs and roofed the house of one of the local cops, who agreed to look the other way if they did the job cheap.

"They both do it," he says, "and they wanted Sherly to try what they had just made up. I knew why she was going," he said, "but I couldn't stop her. No matter what I said or how much I begged and promised, she wasn't listening to me. I watched as she slid in the back seat of the old Cutlass they drove. Her hand was out the window and waving as the car moved away from the curb, down 25th street, and out of sight.

"I'm heartsick," he says. "I can't sleep, I can't eat and I haven't been out of the house in days. It was late afternoon when I got the call that said she was dead. Dead just a few blocks from my house. She was hit by a train after sitting on the tracks. Her body was dragged from 25th Street about two miles to the edge of town before the train got stopped. Suicide, they called it.

"The train conductor said he could see her slumped on the tracks not moving, but the train was going too fast to stop. Her body was spread over a few hundred yards of train tracks.

Blood, hair, human tissue, all up and down the tracks. There was no way to identify any shot marks on her neck from what was left of her body. The train conductor said he blew the whistle over and over, but she wouldn't, couldn't and didn't move. She didn't flinch with the train whistle because she was already dead before she got hit and ran over. It seems New Castle is a hub of train death as preferred cover-up.

"It was reported that someone helped her get out of the vehicle thought to be owned by her brother and onto the tracks. She didn't walk to the tracks and sit down; she was dumped onto the tracks by two people who were seen getting back in an older car and driving away. She was left there dead after she was injected in the neck with a methamphetamine concoction by her brother and sister-in-law.

"They gave her a 'hot shot' to get high, but it killed her instead. When they discovered she was not just high she was dead, they wrapped her body in a big black overcoat and put it on the tracks. Making it look like she killed herself, to avoid getting in trouble. She wasn't depressed and I don't believe she would kill herself," he says. "She was a young beautiful woman in the prime of her life with grandchildren she adored. She would not have done that to us," he said.

"My sister-in-law confessed to me at the funeral," he goes on to say. He is now crying minimally into his hands that are clasped over his face. "She came up to me to express her condolences and blurted out that they didn't mean to kill her. They just wanted to give her a quick pick-me-up, she said. 'I didn't know what happened; when I gave it to her, she couldn't handle it,' she went on to say. 'Deena seemed to keep mumbling; I didn't know it would hurt her, I wanted to help her feel good and be happy,' she said.

"These people are crazy," he says. "I have been around them when they party and seen them do some strange stuff. I was there once when her brother Ritchie was so wasted on drugs that he was eating out of an ashtray with a spoon thinking it was his plate of food.

"I've seen them snort the ashes of a dead body because they thought it was crushed up Xanax. This girl I have never seen before, walked in the house during one of their parties, she had one of those little container keepsakes on her keyring. You know the ones that people carry their loved one's ashes in as a keepsake. Well, when she got up to go to the bathroom, she left her keys on the coffee table and they opened that thing and passed it around, snorting the contents. It was nuts!

"Ritchie still had it in is hand, closing the lid when she walked in the room. She started laughing and said, 'How did my husband taste?! You just snorted his ashes.' They're out there," he says. "Who knows what they would do to me if they got messed up and wanted revenge or something? I can't tell anyone what they did to her," he says, "I just can't I'm afraid. I'm afraid they will try to blame me and say that I am the one who killed her out of jealously because she was so much younger than I am. It might be better to let people believe she killed herself, I don't know," he says. "I just don't know!"

Chapter 16
Ruined Lives

Mr and Mrs Tapping are your average hard-working couple. He was a security guard and she was a childcare worker. They also owned and ran a local bait and tackle shop for many years in the area. It's one mile from the entrance to a state park with year-round fishing, camping, boating and a beach area. When they decided to sell out, they did so to what they thought was another honest hardworking citizen who happened to be on the Blue River school board, so they expected nothing but the truth. This man dealt with the lives of children on a routine basis, so you would expect him to be morally sound. Turns out, he was far from morally anything in his dealings with Mr and Mrs Tapping.

Mr Smith and the Tappings arranged a deal that would allow him to take over the mortgage payment of the bait and tackle shop. The mortgage itself would remain in Mrs Tapping's name. Mr Smith paid his down payment, that consequently all went to the mortgage company, and took over the bait and tackle shop as decided. He began to make changes around the shop as you would expect – a new owner making change and putting personal touches on the business.

He soon started to dig up the fuel cells and gas pumping station that was part of the business and property. He did not replace, improve or modify the portion of the property that was a gas station and part of the bait and tackle shop. Instead, this portion of the business was no longer functional, so selling gas on the property was no longer a viable asset.

He then started to remove and remodel the outdoor storage buildings that were used to store boats in the winter and supplement the income of the bait shop during the winter months and down seasons. He did not replace the storage buildings with bigger or better units, he simply got rid of them and part of the bait shop income.

He proceeded to allow the inside of the shop to become rundown with broken and malfunctioning freezers, water units that held life bait, and refrigeration units.

Six months into the sale of the bait and tackle shop, Mrs Tapping found herself once again making the payments. Payments on the mortgage to avoid ruining her credit, as Mr Smith stopped making payments like he was supposed to and as he agreed upon in the contract between the two. Mr Smith would not make the payment and he would not take calls from the mortgage company. Furthermore, he avoided the calls and visits of Mrs Tapping when she tried to reach out to him or went to his home.

Once Mrs Tapping was finally able to surprise Mr Smith in a public place, he had no choice but to speak to her. He immediately gave her the keys to the bait and tackle shop and said he could not make any money and wanted out of the deal. He did not offer explanation as to why he had eliminated the fuel cells and the inability to sell gas, nor did he explain why he rid the property of valuable storage units that brought in profit to the bait and tackle shop.

Mr and Mrs Tapping were beside themselves as now they had the same mortgage but a ruined business that had thrived under the management of the Tappings.

The stress was so great that Mr Tapping began to become mentally overwhelmed, leading to psychosis that has not totally resolved. Psychosis that is now something he will live with and take medication to control the rest of his life.

Mr Tapping started to have problems at his job, he refused to allow the president of the company in his own building thinking it was a trick and he would get fired if he did. He started to take the clocks in the home apart to see if he was being watched and monitored. He took the bulbs out of the lights in the home, for psychosis made him believe they were listening to him. He no longer left his home and when he did, he rushed to get back thinking he was being followed. Mr Tapping had become so paranoid that his last day of work he drove home at a speed greater than 100 miles per hour, getting him a traffic ticket and a state police escort home. He simply told the state police that he was being followed and was trying to get away from the unknown person following him and that he was afraid to stop.

The stress and the financial burden on Mr and Mrs Tapping had gotten so great, their credit was in jeopardy of being ruined. The mental stress had caused Mr Tapping to become psychotic and he was ultimately institutionalised for months.

Mrs Tapping retained several local attorneys who took her money up front. Two thousand dollars here and two thousand dollars there, but in the end, none of the retained lawyers were able or willing to help her as they are friends of or acquainted with Mr Smith. The local judge refused to help Mrs Tapping as he too is a friend of Mr Smith and enjoys days at the local fair, judging pigs with his friend Mr Smith, another of the good ole boys.

I suggested an out-of-town attorney to avoid the good ole boy network of Henry County, Indiana. Mrs Tapping did in fact get an attorney from another city who is suing Mr Smith for damages. He is pursuing the case with very little retaining fee as he realises the financial problems the Tappings have endured.

At first Mr Smith tried to avoid the new legal actions and the new out-of-town attorney by simply not returning calls, responding to correspondence and not signing for certified mail. Once subpoenaed by the outside attorney, he had no choice; Mr Smith had to respond. Mrs Tapping retains the photographs of the damage that was done by Mr Smith; the same photographs the local judge chose to ignore.

The new attorney, who is not in bed with the local judicial system, has made it possible for Mr and Mrs Tapping to get a settlement from Mr Smith, holding him accountable for the property destruction, the mental anguish and personal losses of the Tappings. Mr Smith was never going to be held responsible for the damage he had done to the Tappings if they had not sought after counsel outside the good ole boy network of Henry County, Indiana.

Chapter 17
Not Such a Casanova Cop

It's 3:30 Monday afternoon and the local high school is soon letting out for the afternoon. It's mid to late summer so the dress code of students is lax, and comfort is the theme in the hot weather. Miniskirts, thin T-shirts, shorts and tank tops that meet the minimal dress standards of the local high school are the norm for the young female students. A high school that has become more interested in accolades for graduating 100% than quality of education, attendance or student safety.

Little do they know they are being watched, discussed and rated from across the way by a uniformed pervert. Scooter Cop cannot seem to get a date with someone his own age as he is less than attractive to the women he pursues. He suffers alopecia, is continuously dishevelled in appearance, and speaks as if he is a teenage boy instead of a grown-up man.

His police cruiser is parked directly in front of the high school, slightly hidden by the foliage of the local park that is only a few feet away from the high school main entrance. He sits in his police cruiser watching hundreds of unassuming young girls exit from school that afternoon.

This is Scooter Cop's preferred way to pick up women, but they are not at all women, they are only little girls. Scooter prefers the young ladies, he says they have a built-in Brazilian wax to their tight little pussies, as he often says and laughs when he shares his tasteless stories with his buddies in and out of the police department. He brags of his encounters with these young teenage girls as if he has nothing to fear and his molestation tendencies will never be found out or he is oblivious that the friends he shares his stories with share them also and find his actions disgusting.

Scooter Cop has targeted and manipulated dozens of girls as they leave the school parking lot. He follows them, learns their routine, stalks their movements and then strikes when he feels he has obtained all the information needed to blackmail these girls for sex if they get into any type of trouble. Trouble he will ultimately cause so he can molest them. Knowing they do not want their parents to find out so they will not speak a word of it, as he pressures these young ladies by following them from school, parking close enough for them to see his presence at their homes, and boldly speaking to their parents in their presence when possible. Ensuring his well-meaning actions of protect and serve that are his cover for molestation.

Scooter Cop also targets the younger population of women who happen to have any type of offense, traffic, drug or any type of legal issue. He will fix the problem for a blowjob and the off chance to be their first experience with anal sex. As Scooter Cop is fascinated with anal sex so much, you might question his sexuality. Maybe the macho cop image will not allow him to admit or live the lifestyle he prefers.

Scooter is known by his friends and those around aware of him as not being of very high moral content but of hedonistic behaviour instead. He often touts his behaviour to anyone who will listen as he seems proud of his actions. Yet Scooter Cop, known to harass, manipulate and take advantage of young women, remains unscathed by his actions. Is he hidden in plain sight behind his police uniform? Is he protected by his cohorts and a bond they share to protect one another regardless of their actions?

Scooter Cop picks his target, a young red-haired, freckle-faced innocent making her way to her car after the rush of students has calmed. She is at least 16 as she drives to school. Scooter identifies her car as a small, bright yellow Volkswagen (VW) Beetle convertible with flowers on the brake lights and eyelashes on the headlights. A sweet one he is thinking and notices he is salivating by just watching her every movement. She is wearing tasteful knee-length white shorts that fit tight to her trim and taut body. Scooter notices the outline of her behind and again starts to salivate. His target has on plain white sneakers and a blue sleeved shirt she has rolled up to her elbows and tucked into her shorts. She obviously has it all together, this unsuspecting young lady. She is carrying only a few books that are held in the crook of her right arm. She has a small pink purse draped over her head, around the left side of her neck, and resting on her right hip.

"She's my next victim," Scooter says to himself. Young and sweet, hopefully with daddy issues, and a good girl mentality – never wanting to disappoint her parents! "My kind of girl," he says again, but this time he is speaking to the air in his police cruiser as he sits and stalks his prey.

She pulls away from the almost empty parking lot and Scooter Cop is quick to get behind her and jot down her license plate number. "Well, that will be easy to remember!"

he says grinning a sinister smile, eyes open wide as if they will protrude from his head when he reads the words DDYsGrL. "Perfect," Scooter Cop says to himself and cackles a loud boisterous laugh that seems to consume him for several minutes as he follows the innocent young lady who will become his next victim.

Scooter continues to follow close behind the yellow VW until it pulls slowly into the driveway of a minimalist white single-storey home on the corner of Elm and 7th street. Her home is only a few blocks from the local police station and Scooter Cop's own home on 10th and Elm. Why has he never noticed her before, he wonders to himself as he drives past the house to the end of the block and turns to go back to the local high school where he will spend the next few hours watching the girls' tennis team practice as he masturbates in his police car. He pleasures himself while skulking at the young girls on the tennis court with their short skirts that fly up over their bottom and their bouncing breasts as they run and jump for the ball.

Minutes after she is sure he is gone and no longer following her, Cindy (the young lady he has decided to prey upon) pulls back out of the driveway on 7th and Elm and heads home. "Whew," she sighs, relieved he did not stop and summon her to his car as he has so many of the girls she goes to school with. Cindy is a high school senior and is aware of the perverted policeman as he is known to her and her friends at school. Seems Scooter forgot how much young girls gossip and chat among themselves. Cindy continues home to her house at the edge of town. Her home is secured with an iron fence as her father is the executive officer of his metal working company and does well for himself and his family.

Cindy quickly enters the code and pulls into the long drive as the gates close behind her. She is safe at home now.

The first thing she does is text her group of girlfriends to tell them of the incident and being followed by the perverted cop. Unbeknownst to Scooter, Cindy is aware of him and his stalking behaviour, and she and her girlfriends have devised a plan to protect themselves from his unwanted advances and stalking behaviour. Cindy is barely 17 and has two older brothers who are now in college and a younger sister aged 15 who attends the same high school but always takes the bus home at her father's direction. 'He got behind me just as I left the school parking lot,' she texts to her friends. 'I drove as I normally do and made sure not to give him a reason to pull me over,' she continues. Cindy continues to text, 'I pulled into a driveway on the other side of town that looked empty with someone out on the sidewalk a few houses down from where I stopped. I pulled up close to the garage and turned my car off as he drove on past the house. I could see him laughing and looking my way, he's such a creep,' Cindy texts her friends. 'I was shaking so bad,' she continues to text to her friends. 'Once I saw him turn the corner and get out of sight, I backed out and went the other way. I was shaking all over,' Cindy texts to her friends.

'Are you telling your dad?' one of the girls text back.

'Yes, I most certainly am as soon as he gets home from work,' Cindy texts back. 'Remember, we made a pact to tell our parents about him and what he has done and does to young girls at school. I don't want the same thing that happened to Melissa to happen to me,' Cindy texts her friends.

'Me either,' several of the girls chime in with a text. 'Bald perv,' one of the girls texts, 'why won't he leave us alone.'

Another chimed in, 'Because he thinks nobody knows about that girl getting pregnant by him and him taking her out of state for an abortion or the way he chases after young kids.'

Melissa chimed in just then, 'Cindy, I am so glad you got away from him, he's crazy.'

'I think he knew my dad was dead, and I was alone. That's why he hounded me so much,' Melissa texts. 'There was nobody to do anything about it. I am the foster kid of another cop who is an alcoholic and his wife is so friggin' religious, she wouldn't believe me when I told her what he was doing. But I have heard on Facebook and stuff that he does the same thing to women he pulls over, picks up for drugs and junk. He's gross, with that greasy bald head that shines and dirty fingernails. He's got to stalk because nobody wants him!' They all chime in: 'LOL.'

'Melissa, I'm sorry for what happened to you,' Cindy texts. 'Me too,' all the girls join in with tear and shocked emojis expressing emotion to the horror.

'It was bad,' Melissa texts back. 'He used to follow me home from school and stop me on the sidewalk to talk. He asked me all kinds of questions, says he knew how it was to lose your parents. He would drive by and if I was at home on the porch, he would bring me back stuff like food, a milkshake, or little stuffed animals,' she texts her friends.

'Wow,' someone texts.

'I was only 12 when he started paying me all that attention, I didn't know what was happening until it was too late,' Melissa texts to her friends. A crying emoji comes across the screen of her phone from one of her friends and she texts back, 'It's ok, it's over now, but I don't want him to do it to anyone else and get away with it.

'He would come over when my foster father was home and pretend to be interested in something he was saying, all the while he would be looking me up and down. My foster dad was drunk most of the time and didn't even notice what was going on. The first time they left me alone with him was a nightmare,' she texts to her group of friends. 'They wanted to go out on a date night like he suggested they do, to do something for themselves after working and fostering me and stuff,' she text. 'The pervert cop offered to look after me while they were out that night. He told my dad he would drive by and be sure everything looked OK! Drive by my ass,' she texts her friends. 'He must have watched them leave the house because not five minutes after they left and I locked the doors, he was there.

'I remember it like it was yesterday, I just can't seem to forget,' she texts her group of friends. 'He had a McDonald's bag in his hand with a Coke in the other. He was in his police car and left it parked out front of the house and not in the driveway. I wish I had never opened the door,' Melissa texts her friends. 'Once he was inside, he sat the Coke down on the table by the door. He pulled a big wad of brown napkins from the bag and dropped the bag in the floor beside where he stood at the entryway. He turned from me and shut the door behind him and locked it, and I knew then I was in trouble,' she texts. 'He grabbed me by the arm and pulled me close to him; he smelled like cigarettes and something stale or moulded, I couldn't tell what it was – it almost made me puke. His clothes were all wrinkled up. He's gross,' she texts.

'Melissa, did you scream?' one of her friends texts back.

'No, I couldn't do anything, he stuffed that handful of napkins from the bag in my mouth and put handcuffs on me.

My arms were behind me and he was pushing me toward the living room. I couldn't do anything but kick and try to get away. I remember he was laughing and making creepy noises, his face was red, and his nose was running, it was sickening and scary. He kept talking to himself, saying stuff like she's a fresh one and nobody will ever believe her against me. I was crying and coughing, getting choked on the dry napkins getting wet and falling apart in my mouth. He just kept pushing me and making noises, until we were in the living room and he rammed me into the back of the couch,' she texts her friends. 'I was bent over the couch on my belly and he was rubbing up against me, moaning.'

'OMG!' her friends text back.

'That's not the worst of it,' she starts texting her friends again. 'He started grabbing me, pulling at my boobs and pinching my nipples, it hurt!' she texts. 'He was lying on top of me bent over the back of the couch, he was rubbing up against my butt, grabbing and pulling my nipples, moaning and groaning the whole time. He pulled my pants down and took my bra and panties off. He kept ramming his hands in my butt, it was awful, it hurt so bad!'

'EWW!' someone text back.

'That's not even the worst of it, he kept one hand up my shirt, pulling my breast and pinching my nipples and the other he had in my crotch, scratching me and rubbing me with his hands. He stuck his fingers inside of me and kept cursing, calling me names.'

'What did he call you?' someone texts asking.

Melissa started to text back, 'He kept calling me bitch and cunt, that kind of stuff, it was awful! After he got my panties down, he started taking his belt off and I started shaking so bad, I kept trying to scream and would get choked on the napkins. Before I knew what was happening, he had stuck his thing inside me, and it hurt. I kept crying and he kept pushing at me, slamming into me and moaning, calling me names and pulling my hair. It was awful, he was grunting and slobbering, kissing my back and my neck, pulling my nipples and rubbing my breast so hard. He kept doing that for a while,' Melissa text her friends, 'and then he grabbed both my breasts in his hands and smashed them, crammed himself even closer to me and pushed me, leaning over the couch even more. I could feel him then with one hand grab my butt and rub it. He jammed his dick in my butthole and I jumped forward, it hurt me so bad,' Melissa texts her friends. 'He kept ramming his dick in me and smashing my boobs. It was a nightmare. When he was done, he shivered and laughed as he pulled away from me. That smell was there again, that smell I didn't know what was.'

'Oh, Melissa,' someone texts, and everyone texts: 'I'm sorry' throughout the group.

Melissa started texting again. 'He pulled me by the hair and grabbed the napkins from my mouth. He told me to go shower and give him my clothes. He cleaned up the couch with some kind of cloth he had with him and acted like nothing had ever happened.

'He watched me shower and took my clothes when he left. He grabbed my hair again and said if I tell, he would get my dad the drunk fired and my mom, the Christian, would not believe it anyway. I locked the door when he left and went to my room and cried myself to sleep. It was awful!' Melissa text her friends.

'I'll bet he did the same thing to that girl who got pregnant and he took her to get an abortion,' someone in the group text.

'He is sickening,' Melissa texts. 'Cindy, tell your dad what he did,' urged Melissa in a last text and the girls ended their call.

Chapter 18

Thoughtless Son

Did the son of a local state representative get away with murder, hit and run as well as drunk driving because conveniently his car was cleaned of all evidence?! Leaving the local Elks Lodge from a night of drinking and partying, young Lyle got behind the wheel drunk. He pulled away from the curb and proceeded onward, not thinking of anything but himself as he drove recklessly all over the road on his way south out of town. He lived only a few miles away in another adjacent small town and was sure he could make it home without incident. He was in his father's car and knew he would not get hassled by the local police.

While another unsuspecting young man, Christopher, was walking home from the local all-night gas station after working the evening shift. Christopher was walking south as well and walking along the sidewalk when he was struck from behind by the drunk-driving Lyle. The drunken Lyle continued to make his way home while Christopher lay beside the road dying. Consequently, Christopher did succumb to his injuries from the hit and run and did in fact die at the hands of a drunk-driving Lyle, who fled the scene.

Lyle was driving his father, the state representative's car when the accident happened. Witnesses were able to identify the car as that of Representative Sanderson and the driver as Lyle, his son.

When police went to question and arrest young Lyle, the car had gone missing for a short period of time just before the arrest. A close family friend of the representative who also served as a local bail bondsman had parked the car in his family garage for safe-keeping, nonetheless! Well, the bail bondsman and the representative were rumoured to have cleaned the car of any traces of blood or other fibres that may have identified Lyle as the driver! They got away with drunk driving, hit and run, and tampering with evidence, because Christopher was not the son of a state representative or any other prominent city or local official. And morals seem to be lacking within the community as discussed in all the previous stories! Christopher's life was valued as less than that of drunken Lyle Sanderson, son of State Representative Sanderson. If the people who make the rules cannot seem to follow them, what does this say about the local thought processes?! I can get away with anything I want. Drunk driving to any other individual is a serious matter by itself, but add vehicular homicide and jail time is expected from regular folks in the community. Why was the court system and local law enforcement so complacent with this hit and run drunk driver? You or I would have been imprisoned! Detachment from the community they serve, corruption and indifference seem to be the personality of the egos who continue to behave as if they are indispensable.

The End

18-year-old Mooreland man killed when struck by train

Curtis Wayne Wagner, attended Blue River schools

Curtis Wayne Wagner, 18, of rural Mooreland died Sunday morning from injuries sustained in a train-pedestrian accident.

He was born Nov. 30, 1973, in New Castle, and was a life resident of Henry County. He attended Blue River schools and also attended the First Church of the Nazarene.

He is survived by his foster parents, Leonard and Ruby Morrison of rural Mooreland; three sisters, Cindy Stegner of New Castle, Donna Waters of Pine Knott, Ky. and Percilla Wagner of Springport; seven brothers, Randy Wagner, James Wagner and Kenneth Wagner, all three of Muncie, Jeff Wagner of rural New Castle, Ronnie Wagner of Richmond, Troy Wagner of New Castle, and Lewis Dale Wagner of Springport; maternal grandmother Marjorie Wilson of Kennard; several aunts, uncles and cousins.

Services will be 10:30 a.m. Wednesday at Macer-Hall Funeral Home with the Rev. Paul Ellis officiating. Burial will follow in South Mound Cemetery.

Friends may call from 4 to 8 p.m. Tuesday at the funeral home.

Aug. 11, 1991

Incident Number: 91-12307
Nature: Deceased Person   Case Number: Image:
    Addr SR 3 / Prairie   Area: PRA   Prarie Townshi
    City: New Castle   ST: IN Zip: 47362   Contact: Rex A Lamar

+-- Complainant: 14523 --+
| Lst: Norfolk & Southern   Fst: Mid: |
| DOB: / /   SSN: Adr 8111 Nelson |
| Rac: Sx: Tel: (260)493-5381 Cty: Fort Wayne   ST: IN Zip: 46805 |
+--+

    Offense Codes: DBOD   Reported: Observed:
    Circumstances:
  Rspndg Officers: P Adams
  Rspnsbl Officer: K Cronk 3318   Agency: HCSO   CAD Call ID: C91-12307
      Received By: J Guy   Last RadLog:
     How Received: T Telephone   Clearance:
    When Reported: 04:03:00 08/11/1991   Disposition: INA Disp Date: 08/12/1991.
  Occurrd between: 04:03:00 08/11/1991   Judicial Sts:
             and: 04:03:00 08/11/1991   Misc Entry: INV
  MO:
   Narrative: (See below)
  Supplement:

* *

INVOLVEMENTS:
Type Record #   Date   Description   Relationship
NM   90-1690   08/28/1991 Wagner, Curtis   Victim
NM   C894   08/18/1991 Frame, Mark L   Coroner
NM   12482   08/18/1991 Wainscott, Thomas M   Asst Officer
NM   18533   08/18/1991 Ward, Bill   Asst Officer
NM   90-2296   08/18/1991 Robinson, Terry L   Asst Officer
NM   90-3063   08/18/1991 Cronk, Kim Lee   Investigating
NM   15585   08/17/1991 Steussy, Helen F   Pathologist
NM   26708   08/13/1991 Carter, Judy J   Assist
NM   26670   08/12/1991 Lamar, Rex Allan   Contact Person
NM   14523   08/11/1991 Norfolk & Southern,   *complainant
CA   C91-12307 08/11/1991 <Not on file>   *initiating Call

LAW Incident Offenses Detail:
               Offense Codes
Seq Code   Amount
  1 DBOD Dead Body   0.00

LAW Incident Responders Detail
    Responding Officers
Seq Name   Unit
  1 P Adams

MT:91x12307   plain   Jan 11, 1990
16:40   Aug 18, 1991   02:17   \\\\\\1\\\\\\\\\\\\\\\\y\\\\\\
\\\\

\\PLAIN
\\ Henry County Sheriff's Department - Incident Narrative Report\

\The following facts and information subscribed and sworn\
\to before me this
\\\date: ===================================
===================\
\ On August 11,1991 on or about 02:28AM I, Deputy Paul R Adams of
\\\the Henry County Sheriffs Department was dispatched to a criminal
\\\mischief in progress in Mechanicsburg area, I, Adams, at the time
\\\of the dispatch was in the area of CR300S and SR3.\

\ As I, Adams, entered Mt.Summit I noticed a vehicle sitting
\\at a southwest angle to the fuel pumps on the south side of
\\the Marathon Station, The vehicle had two occupants and the
\\\headlights were off but the park lights were on, this being
\\\unusual I, Adams, stopped to check the occupants. The occupants
\\\were familiar to this officer and were awaiting he arrival of
\\\another friend. The time for this was approx. 02:35AM\

\As I, Adams, started to leave the station a small red vehicle
\\pulled just past the front of my patrol vehicle and a large
\\white male subject exited the vehicle and approached my vehicle
\\\requesting to speak to me. The man identified as Rex A Lamar of
\\\Hagerstown stated that on or about 02:10AM the same date he had
\\overheard radio traffic on his portable hand held scanner in
\\his vehicle that a train that had passed through the area had
\\\observed an "Unidentifiable object on the tracks in the area of
\\\CR400N and SR3".\

\I, Adams, explained to Lamar that all units were busy on calls
\\\and that I too, was in route to the criminal mischief in progress
\\\but as soon as a unit was able that the area would be checked. I,
\\\Adams, arrived in Mechanicsburg approximately 02:43AM\
\and was unable to locate any mischief, I, Adams, cleared the call
\\\at approximately 02:49AM and proceeded to the Mt Summit Area to
\\\check the tracks. Upon my arrival in the area I, Adams, checked
\\\the tracks north and south of US36 with the overhead "alley
\\\lights" on my vehicle, I, Adams, then proceeded to the area
\\of Prairie Rd. and checked the tracks northwest and southeast,
\\1, Adams, then proceeded to CR400N and checked northwest and
\\\southeast still not observing any articles.\

\I, Adams, then went north on SR3 to check a vehicle in the median
\\\just south of the US36 overpass, as I, Adams, approached the

\\vehicle it was noticed that it was just turning around and had
\\newspaper delivery markings on the rear, I, Adams, then proceeded
\\to the area of CR300N and SR3 to check the tracks north and
\\south, as I, Adams, entered on the tracks on CR300N I was advised
\\by the dispatcher to meet with railroad personnel at SR3 and
\\Prairie Rd. in reference to a deceased person found on the
\\railroad tracks, the time of this call was approximately 03:03AM.\

\As I, Adams, arrived at the scene I was greeted by railroad
\\personnel Daryl Daffron and Bruce Stacey whom stated that they
\\were dispatched to the area to identify an unknown article on the
\\tracks, upon their arrival they observed a young white male lying
\\on his right side between the rails of the tracks a few yards
\\north of the intersection, Both Stacey and Daffron led me to the
\\area of which they noticed the body, I, Adams, then proceeded
\\to the body and checked the carotid pulse of which none was
\\apparent, also the body was cold and clammy and the visible blood
\\was dried.\
\
\At this point I, Adams, requested the dispatcher to dispatch
\\Detective Kim Cronk, Coroner Mark Frame, Photographer Mike
\\Bond and K&W Ambulance service to the scene, Approximately ten
\\to fifteen minutes later officers Thomas Wainscott and Terry
\\Robinson of the Middletown Police Department while in route to
\\Middletown from New Castle stopped to assist. Approximately five
\\minutes after Wainscott and Robinson arrived officer Bill Ward
\\arrived to the scene followed by detective Kim Cronk.\
\
\I, Adams, then began to take measurements which are as follows\
\
\   (A) From the apex of the north rail and west edge of SR3 to
\\\   the center of the victims head 608 feet\
\
\   (B) From REMC pole #475 located on the east side of Prairie
\\\   Rd. north of SR3 to the victims head 175 feet\
\
\   (C) From the apex to the pole #475 653 feet\
\
\I, Adams, then gave all information obtained to Detective Cronk
\\\and proceeded to the Hospital.\
\
\
\This Report for records purposes and Detective Division and
\\Coroners Office\
\
\ 08/12/91 Deputy Paul E Adams Henry County Sheriffs Department\
\===\
\
\x On Monday 8.12.91 around 10 am an autopsy was performed at the
\\\Henry county memorial hospital morgue.\
\The victim was a white male identified as Curtis Wagner, Mr.
\\\Wagner was struck by a Norfolk and Southern train in the early
\\\morning hours of Sunday the 11th of August 1991 south of MT
\\\Summit in the area of SR3 and CR400N.\
\The attending physician at the autopsy was Dr. Helen Steussy, the
\\\Pathologist at the Hospital. Assisted by Judy Carter also a\

member of the Hospital staff.\
Also present was myself, Dep. Thomas and Dep. Fox of the Henry
County Sheriff Department. Our duties were for Dep. Fox to take
photographs of the victim and his injuries and my duties were to
take notes and to be advised by Dr. Seussy of the cause of death.\
Upon my arrival I observed the victim to be a white male age of
18. The victims name was Curtis Wagner. His visible injuries were
as follows;\
Starting at the head , he had a long laceration to the top of his
head , above the hair line and above the right eye. A laceration
above the right ear and in the brow and eye lid area of his right
eye. He had another laceration on the left side of his head close
to his temple and abrasions to the right side of his face from
his jaw to above the forehead and across his right eye area.\
The left arm and shoulder area had multiple abrasions and
lacerations , also the top of the right hand had lacerations on
it. These were later determined to be secondary injuries caused
when he had possibly landed after being struck by the train.\
The right arm and shoulder area had multiple abrasions and
lacerations. Also the left hand had small lacerations on it
to. These injuries were possibly caused by the fall after being
struck by the train.\
The right buttocks area had 4 different spots of abrasions.\
Injuries to the left side of the body were that area of the back
from the small of the back to the shoulders. Multiple contusions
and abrasions especially in the area midways from the shoulder to
the buttocks and to the area just left of the spine.\
This particular area is where Dr. Steussy believes impact with
the train occurred. The head injuries could have occurred from
the fall after being hit by the train.\
During the autopsy to confirm Dr. Steussy's earlier statement
it was discovered that internal injuries to the body's organs
consisted of;\
damage(tear) to the left lung , massive damage to the spleen ,
and a tear in the left rear side of the heart. These were caused
by the ribs in the area of the 10th and 11th being fractured and
puncturing those organs. The kidneys on the left side of the body
were also damaged from what Dr. Steussy termed as deceleration
injuries. This occurs when the body is suddenly stopped or the
motion is reversed. This causes traumatic damage by tearing ,
and bruising of the internal organs. \
The rib cage suffered extensive damage by the deceleration.
Multiple ribs had been fractured.\
From the area of the injuries , the victim had to be #1 standing
and or walking on the tracks in the area just to the right of the
center of the train. #2 Had to have been possibly looking back
towards the train , (turned in a counter clockwise movement) , or
#3 walking onto the tracks from an angle.\
No information on the results of the alcohol and or drug tests
are available at this time. Dr. Steussy would have the results of
the autopsy and finding at a later date.\
***\

                    6/12/91 x   Chuck Thomas\

```
\\\                          Date    Time    Reporting Deputy\
\                                                            \
\Prosecuting Attorney                 Field Supervisor    53rd
\\\  Judicial Circuit\
\\PLAIN
```

THIS IS TO CERTIFY, THAT OUR RECORDS SHOW:

Decedent's Name: (First) CURTIS (Middle) WAYNE (Last) WAGNER (Suffix)

Date of Death: August 11, 1991

Place of Death: ST. RD. #3 NORTH   City:

Age: 18 YEARS   Marital Status: SINGLE   Gender: MALE

Cause(s) of death: (a) MULTIPLE INTERNAL INJURIES
                            (b) WALKING BETWEEN RAILS ON TRACKS
                            (c) STRUCK BY TRAIN
                            (d)   Other Conditions:

Certified By: MARK L FRAME NEW CASTLE IN

Cemetery: SOUTH MOUND CEMETERY NEW CASTLE IN Disposition Date 08/14/91

Funeral Home: MACER-HALL FUNERAL HOME NEW CASTLE IN

File Date: 08/27/1991   Book: VIII Page: 282 Line: 1   Issued On: 05/19/2006

(Health Officer)

Not all information is available for all years.
Birth Date: 11/30/1973 November 30, 1973 Birth City: Birth State: IN

Occupation: Industry: SSN: Race: WHITE

Address: R.R. #1 City: MOORELAND State: IN

Spouse:

Father's Name(First,Middle, Last, Suffix): LEWIS FRANKLIN Father's BirthPlace:

Mother's Name (First, Middle) MARY J Maiden: WILSON Mother's BirthPlace:

Informant's Name: CINDY STEGNER Inform. Address: Relationship:

Dr. Patricia Vanderpool DNP Family & Internal Practice

Dr. Patricia Vanderpool DNP, MSN, APRN, FNP-BC, ANP-BC, ANPE
1516 Washington Street, New Castle, IN 47362
Phone: 765-836-5047—Fax: 765-891-8171

I Ronald Wagner give Dr. Vanderpool permission to use the information I provided in writing her novel titled "Absolutely Despicable" I am allowing my real name and the name of my brother Curtis Wagner to be used. I have provided Dr. Vanderpool with information including a death certificate, sheriff's report, and obituaries that she is free to use as she determines necessary. I was not paid for any portion of my information; I will not seek any type of compensation for my information now or in the future. I freely give Patricia Vanderpool the right to all of the documents and information I have provided. I Ronald Wagner understand the novel will be published worldwide.

10-8-19

This agreement signed by Ronald Wagner *Ronald Wagner*
And
Dr. Patricia Vanderpool *Patricia Vanderpool*
10-8-19

Certificate of Death Registration
Henry County Health Department
New Castle, Indiana

THIS IS TO CERTIFY, THAT OUR RECORDS SHOW:

Decedent's Name: (First) CURTIS (Middle) WAYNE (Last) WAGNER (Suffix)

Date of Death: August 11, 1991

Place of Death: ST. RD. #3 NORTH City:

Age: 18 YEARS   Marital Status: SINGLE   Gender: MALE

Cause(s) of death: (a) MULTIPLE INTERNAL INJURIES
(b) WALKING BETWEEN RAILS ON TRACKS
(c) STRUCK BY TRAIN
(d) Other Conditions:

Certified By: MARK L FRAME NEW CASTLE IN

Cemetery: SOUTH MOUND CEMETERY NEW CASTLE IN Disposition Date:08/14/91

Funeral Home: MACER-HALL FUNERAL HOME NEW CASTLE IN

File Date: 08/27/1991 Book: VIII Page: 282 Line: 1 Issued On: 05/19/2008

(Health Officer)

Not all information is available for all years.
Birth Date: 11/30/1973 November 30, 1973 Birth City: Birth State: IN

Occupation: Industry: SSN: Race: WHITE

Address: R.R. #1 City: MOORELAND State: IN

Spouse:

Father's Name(First, Middle, Last, Suffix): LEWIS FRANKLIN Father's BirthPlace:

Mother's Name (First, Middle) MARY J Maiden: WILSON Mother's BirthPlace:

Informant's Name: CINDY STEGNER Inform. Address: Relationship: